Recipes for Sweeter Living

Book One: Cookies & Considerations

D0941079

Recipes for Sweeter Living

Book One:
Cookies & Considerations

Cecilia Lortscher

Published By:

Recipes for Sweeter Living
Publishing

Recipes for Sweeter Living
Book One: Cookies & Considerations

First Printing - December 1999

CANADIAN CATALOGUING IN PUBLICATION DATA:

Lortscher, Cecilia
Essays and recipes originally published in the author's column in the
Canmore Leader.

Contents: BK. 1 Cookies & Considerations.

ISBN 0-9686305-0-2 (v.1)

1. Inspiration. 2. Conduct of life. 3. Cookies.
I. Canmore Leader. II. Title.

BJ1595.L67 1999   158.1'28   C99-901514-1

Cover design by:
Recipes for Sweeter Living
Canmore Printcraft

Cover Photograph by:
Pam Doyle

Cookie Photographs by:
Pam Doyle and the staff at the Canmore Leader
Canmore, Alberta

Printed by:
Canmore Printcraft, Canmore, Alberta
McAra Printing Ltd. Calgary, Alberta

Typesetting, Layout, and Design by:
Recipes for Sweeter Living Publishing

This book is dedicated
to my best friend,
God.

(And to cookie lovers everywhere.)

"The nearest way to God leads through love's open door."
Angelus Silesius

Acknowledgments

"You have to do it yourself, and you can't do it alone."
Martin Rutte

I wish to gratefully thank:

Carol Picard, my first editor
(Carol, you gave me the opportunity to fulfill a dream.
How can I say "thank you" for that?)

David Burke, editor, Canmore Leader
(You are the ultimate "cookie monster".
Every time another year rolls around, I ask if I should continue.
Thank you for letting me.)

Pam Doyle, photographer, Canmore Leader
(Thank you for taking many of the cookie photos
throughout the past two years, Pam.
I especially thank you for taking the wonderful photo on the
cover and for allowing me to use it.)

Shari Bishop, publisher, Canmore Leader
And the staff at the Canmore Leader, past and present.
(Thank you for your support.)

Alice Violini, Mountainside Books
(Thank you, Alice, for being a source to bounce ideas off,
an ear to chew on, and a spot to bang my weary head.)

Peter Philip & Isaac Ormstrup
Canmore Printcraft
(Thank you for your endless patience, invaluable help, resourceful ideas
and for reading my mind!!)

My Husband and My Children
(You knew I had to do this. You understood when I hogged the computer,
retreated to my bakeshop and made supper later and later each night, until
we were almost eating it for breakfast. Thank you.)

Everyone who encouraged me along the way, because . . .
"Encouragement is the oxygen of the soul."
Anonymous

Contents

"For every beauty, there is an eye somewhere to see it. For every truth, there is an ear somewhere to hear it. For every love, there is a heart somewhere to receive it."
Ivan Panin

Introduction
Love is Everywhere

When I first saw the photo that is on the cover of this book, it was push-pinned above Pam's Doyle's desk, at the Canmore Leader.

The photograph immediately captured my heart. When I asked Pam if I could use it for my cover, and she said yes, I was ecstatic, but wondered how I would link a photo of a graffitied train to a book brimming with columns, quotes, cookie recipes and black & white newspaper photographs of cookies.

I still haven't really linked the cover photo to the cookies. And I certainly don't have a particular affinity for trains. However, the link between the graffiti on the train and the thesis of this book, was instant. It was a match made in heaven.

To me, it epitomizes and boldly exclaims what I most want to convey through my writing. Via my love for baking cookies, what I most want to convey, is the need for us all to impart, nurture, embrace and discover more love in the world.

If we are willing, we will see that love is everywhere.

It's in whatever we see as the wonders of life and God's creation. It's in the sweeter things in life like the magic and simplicity of a child at play. It's in blowing iridescent bubbles that float almost to heaven. It's in the glow of laughter that tinkles out loud, and in the quiet of a soundless, simple smile.

Love is in splashing through puddles and squishing through mud. Its in making snow angels and it's in believing in angels. It's in tickling the raindrops off a green-spirited tree. It's in watching the magnificence of the rising or the setting sun. It's in the sight of a flower and the flight of a raven. It's in watching the ocean's ceaseless waves, with sand in your toes and the wind in your hair. Love is in the thoughtful contemplation of maneuvering clouds. It's in a freshly baked cookie. It's in a hug.

It's in the sky, the sun, the earth, the plants, the animals and the people. It's in our eyes. It's in our touch and in our voices. It's in our actions, in our thoughts and our intentions. Love is in our hearts, and in our souls.

For longer than I can remember, writing a cookbook was in my heart and soul. Until I began writing my weekly column, I never had a clear picture of what my book would look like, only that it would be. What it has become is a cookbook that is more than a collection of over 125 *great* cookie recipes. It has become a link to a variety of considerations for a more positive, loving and sweeter outlook on life.

It was written to bring a smile, to lighten your day, to instill a positive thought, to make a difference, to change an attitude, to reach a heart, to shed a tear. Whether you read it for the columns, the quotes, the recipes, or just to look at the pictures, with an early morning coffee or as a bedtime snack, I ask that when you read it, you do so with a willingness to see that love is the force that moves our souls.

Read it because, if you are willing to see it, love is everywhere.

Faith is . . . Not Just For Our Darkest Hour

A few weeks ago, the radio alarm clock awoke me to the sounds of an unidentified, male voice, doing a resonating rendition of "Let it snow". Indicative, as it was, of record-breaking lows and near-freezing temperatures, we should have been making preparations for Christmas - but the one in July!

A week later, the radio alarm clock awoke me to the somber news that search crews had recovered the bodies of John F. Kennedy, Jr., his wife, Carolyn Bessette Kennedy and her sister Laurel Bessette, from their plane wreckage off the coast of Martha's Vineyard.

It has often been said that the Kennedy family has a strong sense of faith. No doubt, they will be calling upon it as they mourn their loss and process their emotions and experiences.

While we naturally have a deeper appreciation of faith at Christmas time, our greater challenge to believe comes as our world seems to crumble, as nothing makes sense, as reason for faith seems quiet and far off.

At a memorial service a while back, it was once expressed to me, how difficult it must be for someone to endure the ceremony during their "darkest hour". My reply was misunderstood.

"How do you know it's their darkest hour?"

It's human nature to mind a little bit of everybody's business, especially when our intentions are to reach out and help, but our beliefs and experiences are our own. What we believe, determines our own state of mind, not someone else's. Our expectations of other people to express sorrow are based on our own beliefs.

As well, we sometimes forget that the real issue is not the cause or the depth of our suffering, but our reaction to it. The end of a physical life, a relationship, an illness, a situation where everything seems to go wrong, may be the means for us to alter our focus and change our outlook and direction, and restore our faith.

What is faith? Faith is as individual as we are.

Faith is . . . having a strong belief that when we fall back, we will be caught before we hit the ground.

Faith is . . . knowing there is something sacred to hold onto.

Faith is . . . having courage without fear.

Faith is . . . magnifying the light and reducing the darkness.

Faith is . . . searching for, and drawing on, a strength within.

Faith is . . . striving for a greater awareness.

Faith is . . . accepting God's timing, not giving up, persevering.

Faith is . . . after anger, muddling, tears and pain, knowing there is a future.

Faith is . . . finding new meaning and purpose through suffering, coping and finally joys.

Faith is . . . accepting what is given, rather than dwelling on what has been taken away.

Faith is . . . acceptance, release, understanding, and the energy to move on.

Faith is . . . knowing that sometimes things happen only to strengthen our faith – faith in others, faith in ourselves, faith in what we cannot fully rationalize, embody or perceive.

Faith is . . . comprehending that, when others experience and overcome tragedies greater than ours, because they do, so can we.

Faith is . . . an unexplainable, uncontainable, irreplaceable, invincible, unconditional, irresistible belief that everything will turn out – at Christmas time (in July or December), when we lose a loved one, when we encounter difficult times, and all the time.

Food for Thought:
"Faith is . . . knowing with your heart."
N. Richard Nash

Know!

Cranberry Harvest Oatmeal
Cookies & Considerations
on following page.

Cranberry Harvest Oatmeal Cookies

2 cups flour
1 tsp. baking powder
1/2 tsp. baking soda
1/2 tsp. salt
1 cup butter
1 & 1/2 cups sugar
2 eggs
1 tsp. vanilla
2 cups rolled oats
2 cups Mariani® Harvest Medley (or dried cranberries)
1 & 1/2 cups yogurt or white chocolate chips (optional)

Combine flour, baking powder, baking soda and salt. Set aside. Cream together butter and sugar. Add eggs and vanilla, mixing well. Add flour mixture and oats. Blend in fruit and chips. Drop onto greased cookie sheets.

Bake at 350 for 12 minutes or till lightly browned at edges.

Cookies & Considerations:

Mariani®, makes a great dried mix called "Harvest Medley". It's a blend of sweetened, dried cranberries, orange flavored cranberries, apples, and tart cherries.

Faith is . . . knowing in your heart that Mariani's Harvest Medley® makes these chewy cookies wonderful for Christmas (in July or December) and all the time, but you can use regular dried cranberries if you can't find these ones, or substitute any other type of dried fruit.

Triple Chocolate Biscotti

1 & 3/4 cup flour
2 tsp. baking powder
1/4 cup cocoa powder
1/3 cup butter or margarine
2/3 cup sugar
2 eggs
4 ounces white chocolate, chopped
4 ounces semisweet chocolate, chopped

Combine flour, baking powder, and cocoa powder. Set aside. Beat butter. Add sugar and mix till combined. Beat in eggs. Add flour mixture and chocolate, mixing by hand if necessary. Divide dough in half. Shape each piece into a 9 inch long log. Roll logs in sugar if desired. Place logs 4 inches apart on lightly greased cookie sheet. Flatten slightly to about 2 inches wide.

Bake at 375 for 20 minutes or till done in the center. Cool for 1 hour. Slice diagonally into half-inch thick slices. Lay slices down and bake at 325 for 8 minutes or till biscotti are dry and crisp. Dip ends in chocolate if desired.

Cookies & Considerations:

Biscotti are fun and they don't require concentrated attention. They're not everyone's cup of tea, but they go great with a cup of tea - or a cup of coffee. Try them if you like a good, chocolatey dunker to go with your café latte.

"Lord, take my lips and speak through them; take my mind and think through it; take my heart and set it on fire."
W. H. Aitken

Believe It! The Christmas Spirit Every Day!

On September 21st, 1897, in a letter to eight year old Virginia O'Hanlon, editor Francis P. Church of the New York Sun, answered this classic question: "Is there a Santa Claus?"

Over a century later, Virginia's now famous letter and it's equally eminent reply, continue to express our whimsical need to believe in things we cannot explain. This season, more than any other time of year, we fathom the magnitude of believing in what cannot be seen, touched or proven. I believe the invisible is eternally present and exists despite our skepticism.

"Miracle on 34th Street" couples Virginia in questioning the believability of Santa Claus. In the movie, Santa Claus becomes more than an imaginary figure. He becomes a symbol of the season. He announces that if you can't believe in Santa Claus, you can't accept anything on faith, and are domed to live a life dominated by doubt.

Based on the same principle of belief in the invisible, "Ally McBeal" considers the perceiving of unicorns. As lawyers, they were able to demonstrate that apparitions, and our beliefs, are sometimes based on hope and cannot be proven to be real or pretend, truths or lies, black or white, right or wrong, existent or nonexistent. We have the right to believe in whatsoever we choose.

I believe that, wherever we come from, we deserve freedom - of choice and mistakes, of voice and movement. Freedom from fear.

I believe in our individual abilities to suppress hateful tendencies.

I believe that we are each one-of-a-kind gifts.

I believe that tears and pain can turn into rainbows. I believe that there is joy to be found in sorrow. I believe that there is peace to be found in struggle.

I believe in forgiveness.

I believe that if we follow our dreams, they will come true.

I believe love will heal our world and bring us peace.

I believe in faith. I believe in miracles. I believe that I do not know what the future holds, but I do know who holds the future.

I believe in angels. I believe in unicorns. I believe in Santa Claus.

I believe in the magic of Christmas. I believe that the spirit of Christmas should last throughout eternity and that if we open our hearts, the

Christmas Spirit will carry us through the year.

And I believe in you.

Whether you believe (or not), and what you believe (or not), is your choice. Like Francis, I prefer to throw open the shutters of my mind and fill my heart with love. With little comprehension, but childlike faith, I believe, I believe, I believe! I believe.

Food for thought:
"The most real things in the world are those that neither children nor men can see. . . Nobody can conceive or imagine all the wonders there are unseen and unseeable in the world."
Francis P. Church

Imagine!

Cranberry Spice Chip
Cookies & Considerations
on following page.

Cranberry Spice Chip Cookies

3 & 3/4 cups flour
1 Tbsp. baking soda
1 tsp. salt
1 tsp. cinnamon
1/2 tsp. allspice
1/2 tsp. nutmeg
1/2 tsp. cloves
2 cups butter
1 & 1/2 cups brown sugar
3/4 cup sugar
2 tsp. vanilla
1 cup milk chocolate chips
1 cup white chocolate chips
1 cup dried cranberries

Combine flour, baking soda, salt and spices. Set aside. Cream butter. Add sugars and vanilla, mixing well. Add flour mixture, chips and cranberries. Drop onto cookie sheets and flatten slightly.

Bake at 350 for 12 minutes.

Cookies & Considerations:

I believe that these are my newest favorite cookies. If angels could bake (and I believe they can) I believe they'd make these cookies. Their wonderful, mildly spiced, buttery aroma and sweet, tart taste is angelic. Inhale deeply and derive sublime joy from the luxuriant scent, that emanates as they bake.

This shortbread-like dough looks dry when you begin mixing, so continue beating until it forms a ball.

Coconut Chocolate Oatmeal Cookies

1 & 1/2 cups flour
1 & 1/4 cups rolled oats
1 tsp. salt
1 tsp. baking soda
1 cup butter
1/2 cup sugar
1/2 cup brown sugar
1 tsp. vanilla
1/2 tsp. coconut or almond extract
1 egg
1 cup toasted coconut
8 oz. semisweet chocolate chunks

Combine flour, oats, salt and baking soda. Set aside. Cream butter. Add sugars, vanilla and coconut extract. Add egg and mix well. Add flour/oat mixture. Mix in coconut and chocolate chunks. Drop onto cookie sheets.
Bake at 350 for 12 minutes.

Cookies & Considerations:

This recipe went with a column called "Life is a Banquet - Step up to the Buffet". Their essence will fill the air with a delightful aroma. As it wafts through the house inhale the amazing richness of the combination of coconut and chocolate. Let your sense of smell have a feast before the banquet even begins!

Making Sense of the Senseless

When Alice's rice pudding went missing, I wanted to put out an APB - an All Puddings Bulletin!

The story unfolds as such:

On April 25th, two weeks prior to this Sunday, Mother's Day, at approximately 6 p.m., I brought Alice some rice pudding. Given Alice's new-found severe, food allergies, the rice pudding was meant to help her find something - anything - she could eat.

Anyone who knows Alice knows that she's inclined to wander. She'll often leave a post-it note on her door saying, "Back in 5 minutes." (Sometimes it says 10, 12, or even as much as 15 minutes - but don't time her!)

So, I wasn't surprised, but disappointed, to find the lights on, her car out front and the door locked, with a note on it. I waited a few minutes, then left the rice pudding hanging on the door handle in a reused, innocuous looking, recycled grocery bag. The pudding was - and I'm embarrassed to say this, because you know I like butter better - in a margarine container.

The next day, when I stopped by to inquire after the above mentioned rice pudding, Alice was away. I did the step, pause, step, which Alice's helper, Tim, instantly recognized as the "you aren't Alice" step, pause, step. I explained my mission, but naturally, he knew nothing of the rice pudding.

We collectively deduced that, since it wasn't hanging on the door, Alice had received it. . . until the phone call came!

"Cecilia, I didn't get the rice pudding," Alice said.

I was speechless. Until now.

Who would take Alice's rice pudding, and why? It didn't make sense.

Granted, the demise of the pudding seems somewhat trivial, particularly in light of the recent violence in the schools. I use the pudding only as a small example.

I know that I certainly didn't expect anyone to take Alice's rice pudding. I'm equally certain that the people of Taber and Littleton weren't expecting what happened there. How do we justify someone taking what appears to be someone else's tub of margarine, when, in a nearby community, approximately the same size as ours, people struggle to explain why children take other children's lives?

We can no longer tell our children, "it won't happen here". We can only pray that it doesn't. Obviously, it can happen anywhere.

But how? How could this happen? How did we get to this place, where our attitudes towards guns and violence are so casual and blasé?

In our quest for answers, we try to appoint blame. Home, parents, television, games, the Internet, books, the media and even the classmates fault themselves and/or each other.

In reality, trying to place blame where there is none, trying to justify something that has no justice, trying to explain the unexplainable, answer the unanswerable, and make sense of the senseless, doesn't give us the answers we seek.

In reality, we don't have the answers - merely more questions. Clearly, though, we can agree that a lot of things have to change. We know that we cannot let this go uncorrected.

Fortunately, we all have the power to change what appears to be written in stone.

We change by refusing to accept, and participate, in acts of violence.

We change by showing compassion for other's suffering; by showing goodness, peace, love, forgiveness, respect and comfort; by showing grace, integrity and humility. We change by seeing that the world can be a place of peace, love and light, for the nurturing and indulging of every man, woman and child.

Martin Luther King said, "In our heart is a power more powerful than bullets." In our hearts, we have the power to provide an alternative to hopeless despair. In our hearts, we have the power to contribute to the healing of the world.

That power is love. And sometimes, finding our way back to love may be the only sense we make of something otherwise utterly senseless.

Food for thought:
"Love is the intuitive knowledge in our hearts. . . Love isn't material. It's energy. It's the feeling in a room, a situation, a person. Money can't buy it. Sex doesn't guarantee it. It has nothing at all to do with the physical world, but it can be expressed nonetheless. We experience it as kindness, giving, mercy, compassion, peace, joy, acceptance, non-judgment, joining, and intimacy."
Marianne Williamson

Express!

Rice Pudding
Cookies & Considerations
on following page.

Rice Pudding

4 cups milk
1/2 cup short grain rice
1/2 cup sugar
1/2 tsp. salt
1 tsp. vanilla

1/4 cup whipping cream
cinnamon

Combine milk, rice, sugar, salt and vanilla in a casserole type dish and bake at 325 for 2 & 1/2 - 3 hours, stirring often until the milk has been absorbed and pudding has thickened. Stir in whipping cream. Pour into serving dish and sprinkle with cinnamon.

Cookies & Considerations:

No cookie recipe this week. I wanted, instead, to share my recipe for rice pudding. (Maybe the person who took Alice's can make their own.)

If you make some for your mom this Mother's Day, don't just leave it hanging on her door in a grocery bag, no matter what kind of container it's in! Give it to her in person, if you can, and express your love.

"Lost, yesterday, somewhere between sunrise and sunset,
Two golden hours, each set with sixty diamond minutes . . ."
Horace Mann

Chocolate Chip Coffee Cookies

2 & 1/2 cup flour
3/4 tsp. baking soda
1/2 tsp. salt
3/4 cup sliced almonds, toasted and cooled
1/4 cup instant coffee powder
1 cup butter
1 & 1/4 cup sugar
2 eggs
1 tsp. vanilla
1 - 300 gram package (2 cups) milk chocolate chips

Combine flour, baking soda and salt. Set aside. Dissolve coffee powder in 1 Tbsp. hot water. Set aside. Cream butter and sugar. Add eggs, vanilla and cooled coffee. Add flour mixture. Add chocolate chips and almonds. Drop onto greased baking sheets
Bake at 350 for 10 minutes.

Cookies & Considerations:
A great, soft cookie for the coffee lover in your house.

"When you come to the edge of all the light you know, and are about to step off into the darkness of the unknown, faith is knowing one of two things will happen: There will be something solid to stand on or you will be taught how to fly."
Barbara J. Winter

After a While

Houston, we have a problem.

We're human beings. That's not the problem though. The problem is, we have problems.

The Yiddish word for problems, troubles and worries is "tsouris". For many of us, saying good-bye, especially to a very good friend, is a big "tsouris".

Losing a friend can be like eating a Girl Guide cookie with no filling. It's like no chocolate chips in a chocolate chip cookie. It's like a Smartie® without the colorful candy coating.

Loosing a friend can strike our lives with change. Many of our "tsouris" are due to change and can be associated with one of the following genres: personal growth, change in health or direction, change in relationships, relocation, separation or loss.

Whether we're moving, changing jobs, ending a relationship, watching our children become adults, or losing a friend, it's natural to feel loss, pain and sadness.

Some people seem programmed to revel in change, while others fear and fight it. Sometimes change comes too quickly; sometimes it comes too slowly. Sometimes it is forced upon us; sometimes we bring it upon ourselves. One thing is inevitable. It will come. And when it comes, it can be a stepping stone on the road to learning. With each step and turn, we learn.

After a while, we see that each goodbye can mean the promise of a new beginning, a new adventure, a better job, a more fulfilling relationship, a new connection with our children and even new friends. After a while, we might even come to delight in the adventure that change produces.

And while things change, and people change, it doesn't mean we forget our past. We treasure the memories and learn to find new ways to keep in touch.

After a while, we come to know that true friendship goes beyond time and distance. It's always there - it's the love that fills our hearts.

Food for thought:

"After a while, you learn the subtle difference
Between holding a hand and chaining a soul,
And you learn that love doesn't mean leaning
And company doesn't mean security,
And you begin to learn that kisses aren't contracts
And presents aren't promises,
And you begin to accept your defeats
With your head up and your eyes open
With the grace of a woman, not the grief of a child,
And you learn to build all your roads on today
Because tomorrow's ground is too uncertain for plans.
And futures have a way of falling down in mid-flight.
After a while, you learn
That even sunshine burns if you get too much.
So plant your own garden and decorate your own soul,
Instead of waiting for someone to bring you flowers.
And you learn that you really can endure. . .
That you really are strong.
And you really do have worth.
And you learn and learn. . .
With every goodbye, you learn."
After a While, by Veronica A. Shoffstall

Learn!

Chocolate Candy
Cookies & Considerations
on following page.

Chocolate Candy Cookies

2 & 1/2 cups flour
6 Tbsp. cocoa
1 tsp. salt
1 tsp. baking soda
1 cups butter
3/4 cups sugar
3/4 cups brown sugar
2 eggs
1 tsp. vanilla
1 cup candy coated chocolates
(approx. 4 - 56 gram boxes)
sugar for rolling

Combine flour, cocoa, salt and baking soda. Set aside. Cream butter and sugars. Add eggs and vanilla. Add flour mixture and blend well. Stir in candy coated chocolates. Shape dough into balls and roll in sugar.

Bake at 350 for 12 minutes.

Cookies & Considerations:

Funny or mushy? Which way to go?

"Maxine", the Shoebox Greetings® sweetheart with the bunny slippers, says, "Wish you weren't leaving, you're the least annoying person I know."

We often have friendships that are a treasure and a delight. They go far beyond time and distance. After a while, it's nice to know that our friends, no matter where they are, are with us in spirit.

No matter where you are, stir the candy coated chocolates gently, into these tasty cookies. You don't want to lose any of that colorful candy coating.

Breakfast Cookies

3/4 cup flour
2 cups rolled oats
1/3 cup bran
1 & 1/2 tsp. cinnamon
1/2 tsp. allspice
1/2 tsp. nutmeg
1/2 tsp. baking soda
1/2 tsp. salt
3/4 cup butter or margarine
1/2 cup brown sugar
1 egg
1 tsp. vanilla
1 cup chopped, pitted dates
1 cup grated apple
1 cup walnuts

Combine flour, oats, bran, cinnamon, allspice, nutmeg, baking soda, and salt. Set aside. Cream butter. Add sugar, egg, and vanilla. Add flour mixture. Stir in dates, apple, and walnuts. Drop onto lightly greased cookie sheet, and flatten to about 1/2" thickness.

Bake at 350 for 10 - 12 minutes or till lightly browned.

Cookies & Considerations:

Don't let these cookies distract you by their name. You can eat them any time of the day or night. They're a soft, nutritious, cookie that's naturally low in sugar, and packed with the goodness of oats, bran, and spices, along with great big hunks of dates, apples and walnuts. A great soft cookie. Yum!

Adversity and the Common Cold

As I sit here, my nose is dripping, red and sore. My eyes are burning and watery. My ears are plugged. My breathing is somewhat shallow. My occasional cough has me sipping iced water in the 30-degree heat. My new sultry voice is instantly recognizable as nasal congestion. The physician within me has made a seemingly competent diagnosis. I believe that I have that summer cold that's been going around.

Although the difficulties of adversity can sometimes stimulate us to reach our greatest heights, I will truthfully be grateful enough just to get this column in on time, never mind the greatest heights part. Nevertheless, like sleep and riches, to be truly appreciated, good health must be occasionally interrupted.

There are many times in our lives when something constructive comes out of the invigorating stimulation of adversity. If we call our troubles experiences, and remember that every experience develops some sleeping potential within us, we will feel fortunate and powerful, no matter how adverse our circumstances seem to be.

Like diamonds, people develop under pressure. Our crisis' make us stronger and help us learn more about ourselves. Tough times and our mistakes are great teachers. From them, we learn wisdom for the future. The things that hurt us most, teach us most.

If we think of the times that we've learnt the most, we might see that it is when we have healed our sick selves, after our greatest pain and suffering that we emerge with a stronger soul and a greater awareness. Adversity makes us think. It makes us able to endure. It makes us strong. It makes us feel alive. It makes us feel that we are blessed.

Adversities are often fruitful. Tough times and adverse conditions have generated many a great opportunity for progress. Electricity was discovered because of darkness. A compass was produced due to fog. Exploration came about because of hunger. The value of a job was learnt in the depression.

The better things in life cannot be treasured if we never experience the things they are better than. If we can't endure the bad, we won't know when we have the good. If we've never been unhappy, we won't know when we're truly happy.

Allow yourself to be pushed by the negative, because every situation also has a positive point of view. Cheer for the underdog because, one day, it might be you. When they say that a thing cannot be done, show them that it can.

If we allow it to, opposition, in the form of adversity, can inspire us, improve us, develop our courage and expand our knowledge. The effects can be wonderful.

Food for thought:
"Do not free a camel of the burden of his hump; you may be freeing him from being a camel."
G. K. Chesterton

Cheer!

Oatmeal Raisin
Cookies & Considerations
on following page.

29

Oatmeal Raisin Cookies

3 cups flour
2 & 1/2 tsp. baking powder
2 & 1/2 tsp. baking soda
2 & 1/2 tsp. cinnamon
1 tsp. nutmeg
1 tsp. salt
3 & 3/4 cups rolled oats

1 & 1/2 cups raisins
3/4 cup corn syrup
6 Tbsp. skim milk
3 & 3/4 cups rolled oats (again)

1 cup butter or margarine
2 cups brown sugar
1 cup sugar
3 egg whites
2 tsp. vanilla
2 tsp. maple flavoring

cinnamon sugar for rolling

Combine raisins, corn syrup and milk. Set aside for 5 minutes. In a food processor, grind 3 & 3/4 cups rolled oats. Combine ground rolled oats with flour, baking powder, baking soda, cinnamon, nutmeg, and salt. Set aside. Stir other 3 & 3/4 cups rolled oats into raisin mixture and set aside. Cream butter or margarine and sugars. Add egg whites, vanilla and maple flavoring. Beat in flour-oat mixture, followed by raisin-oat mixture. Drop and roll cookies in cinnamon sugar. Place on greased or parchment lined cookie sheets. Flatten slightly.

Bake at 350 for 12 minutes.

Cookies & Considerations:

As a further challenge, a request was made for a low-fat cookie. These crispy-chewy cookies sparkle like diamonds and have less than half the fat of a regular Oatmeal Raisin Cookie. But no one will ever guess!

Chewy Peanut Oatmeal Cookies

1 & 1/2 cups flour
1 & 1/2 cups whole wheat flour
1 & 1/2 tsp. baking soda
1 & 1/2 tsp. salt
3 cups rolled oats
1 & 1/2 cups butter
1 & 1/2 cups peanut butter
2 cups brown sugar
3 eggs
1 Tbsp. vanilla
1 & 1/2 cups chopped peanuts

Combine flours, soda, salt and oats. Set aside. Cream butter and sugar. Add eggs. Beat well. Stir in peanut butter and vanilla. Mix till smooth. Add flour mixture and mix well. Add peanuts. Drop onto greased cookie sheet and flatten lightly with fork.
Bake at 350 for 12 minutes.

Cookies & Considerations:

I created this recipe by special request for Mary and her children. We can learn from our children while we bake cookies together, and since most kids love peanut butter cookies, they won't even mind that they have the added goodness of whole-wheat flour and oats.

A Bloomin' Labor of Love

The four seasons here (winter, winter, winter and the other season!) don't allow for much blooming time. For some, the struggle to make ends meet denies us the luxury of choosing an occupation in which to bloom. Priority one, is the need to make a buck. No matter how humble the work, the victory comes from a job done well.

For others, it's a matter of forgetting that if love and skill are both present, we can expect life's garden to be in full bloom. Work becomes a labor of love.

When you wake up in the morning, do you still get excited about what you do to earn a living or are you so burnt out, you just roll over and hit the snooze button? Are you interested in what you do to support yourself or are you looking for someone to support you? Are you devoted and committed to the work you're doing or are you almost ready to be committed? Do you know what you have a flair for or do you have to ask a friend what you want to be when you grow up?

Are you already blooming, or are the seeds still germinating between two sheets of wet paper towel? Is there an area where you flower extraordinarily well, or is your garden full of weeds? Does your wisdom shine brightly, or could it use a brisk polish?

Are you working to help beautify, or pollute, the garden of life for yourself, those you love and those you may never meet?

Many of us measure ourselves by what we do to earn a living. Our work gives us a sense of continuity and purpose. At some level, we all need to feel that we are of service to others. We derive pleasure from using our talents and when others appreciate them, we feel special.

Happiness lies partly in finding something we already do very well, that interests us - something our hearts long to contribute to the world. Upon its discovery, and upon putting our entire soul and being into the services that we are equipped to provide, we are able to shine. Hard work, diligence and whole-hearted efforts produce successful results.

What we accomplish in a day, depends on the way we look at and approach our tasks. When we accept all of our jobs, challenging and simple, and wade through them with joy and enthusiasm, miracles can happen. When we work with a dynamic spirit, things get done.

Work we love isn't work. If we pursue our passions, using our talents, abilities and gifts, our special excellence becomes who we really are. Take your own abilities and aptitudes into consideration and success will be certain.

Let others benefit from the fruits and flowers of your acquired wisdom. When we use the energy, ambition and ability that is at our natural resource, the gardens we tend to blossom.

Plant your garden where you already bloom. Plant the seeds of your future and watch your wisdom shine. As you find the meaningful work that you are meant to do, it becomes a labor of love.

Food for thought:
"To love what you do and feel that it matters - how could anything be more fun?"
Katharine Graham

Blossom!

Chocolate, Chocolate Chunk Peanut Butter
Cookies & Considerations
on following page.

Chocolate, Chocolate Chunk Peanut Butter Cookies

2 & 1/2 cups flour
1/2 cups cocoa
1 tsp. baking powder
1 tsp. baking soda
1 tsp. salt
1 cup butter
1 cup peanut butter
1 cup sugar
1 cup brown sugar
2 eggs
2 tsp. vanilla
12 ounces semi-sweet chocolate chunks

Combine flour, cocoa, baking powder, baking soda, and salt. Set aside. Cream butter, peanut butter and sugars. Add eggs and vanilla. Add flour mixture and mix well. Add chocolate chunks. Drop onto cookie sheet and press with a fork.

Bake at 350 for 12 minutes.

Cookies & Considerations:
These fun and easy cookies are labors of love!

*"The best career advice given to the young is
'Find out what you like doing best and get someone to pay you for doing it.'"*
Katherine Whithorn

Almond Crunch Cookies

1 & 1/2 cups flour
1 & 1/2 cups whole wheat flour
6 cups rolled oats
2 tsp. baking soda
1 & 1/2 tsp. salt
1 cup butter
1 cup shortening
2 cups sugar
2 cups brown sugar
2 tsp. vanilla
1/2 tsp. almond flavoring
4 eggs
2 cups toasted, slivered almonds
1 - 300 gram package milk chocolate chips
1 - 225 gram package toffee bits

Combine flour, whole-wheat flour, rolled oats, baking soda and salt. Set aside. Beat butter and shortening. Add sugars and mix till combined. Add vanilla and almond flavorings and eggs; beat well. Add flour mixture. Mix in almonds, chocolate chips and toffee bits. Drop onto greased or parchment lined cookie sheets. Flatten slightly.
Bake at 350 for 12 minutes.

Cookies & Considerations:
These chewy crunchy cookies tend to stick. Parchment paper helps cleanup efforts a lot.

Celebrating Diversity During the Winter Solstice

Evolving over centuries and enduring trials and tribulations and even abolishment, the celebrations we recognize during the winter solstice, have been shaped by many cultures and people.

A legion of varied and diverse observances take place. Altogether, they are steeped in complex history and use rituals and symbolism in their celebrations. In addition to Christmas, two of those observances are Hanukkah and Kwanzaa.

Hanukkah is an eight day, Jewish, mid-winter festival, commemorating the rededication of the Temple in Jerusalem, in 165 BC Like Christmas, Hanukkah marks a single event using rituals and customs from other holidays. More than remembering the miracle of a single drop of oil, Hanukkah is a celebration of the great miracle of survival.

Kwanzaa, a seven day celebration of African-American heritage, resembles the Jewish Hanukkah, with it's candles and duration, and Thanksgiving in tone and theme. While Kwanzaa takes place during the same season as Christmas, it is a non-religious ceremony that strives to promote a feeling of pride and cultural awareness through the exploration of principles. It is not an alternative to Christmas, and many people celebrate both events.

Christmas itself is observed in many different ways around the world. The customs and forms it takes on are based on the diverse rituals that our families develop. Different ethnic groups have their own unique customs and rituals, but common elements unify the importance of Christmas and celebrating the birth of Jesus.

Stockings, midnight mass, mincemeat, Santa Claus, sleighs and reindeer, popcorn and cranberry garlands, ornaments, candles, stars, carols, gift giving, holly and ivy, mistletoe, Christmas cards, Christmas stamps, Yule logs, nativity scenes, and Poinsettias are all part of the diverse range of customs that we participate in at Christmas time.

Our customs, beliefs, faiths and religions, some interrelated, not one of them better than the other, celebrate the winter solstice in diverse ways. Meaningful to our individual heritage, and dwelling peacefully together, they continue to change, to this very day.

* * *

While many Canadians were watching the Calgary Stampeders win the Greycup in 1998, I was developing a new celebration: "Cecilia's Pre-Christmas Greycup Shortbread Challenge".

I baked five different batches of Shortbread cookies and delivered them to some of my neighbors at half time. Their mission, should they choose to accept it (and they did!), was to number, in order of personal preference, their favorites.

The results have been tabulated, but you decide for yourself. If you can't make up your mind, make them all.

Food for thought:
"Before you taste anything, recite a blessing."
Rabbi Akiva

Celebrate!

Shortbread
Cookies & Considerations
on following page.

Shortbread Cookies

1.) Placed: fourth overall (dry)
   1 cup butter
   1/2 cup icing sugar
   2 & 1/2 cups flour

2.) Placed: fifth overall (greasy)
   1 & 1/2 cups butter
   1/4 cup sugar
   dash salt
   2 cups flour

(#3, 4 & 5 were just right.)

3.) Placed: first overall
   1 pound butter
   1/2 cup berry sugar
   3 cups flour

4.) Placed: second overall
   3 cups butter
   1 & 1/2 cups sugar
   1/4 tsp. salt
   7 & 1/2 cups flour

5.) Placed: third overall
   1 cup butter
   1/4 cup sugar
   3 Tbsp. cornstarch
   1/4 tsp. salt
   1 & 3/4 cups flour

In all cases, cream butter and sugar until light and fluffy. Add flour (and other dry ingredients, if listed), beating until mixture holds together. Roll into balls and drop onto cookie sheet. Press with cookie press.

Bake at 300 for 20 minutes or until light golden at edges.

Cookies & Considerations:

Such a simple, traditional cookie, with only 3 basic ingredients. Yet such a richly diverse range of taste, texture and appeal, dwelling peacefully together.

(Betcha can't guess my favorite!)

Miracle Peanut Butter Cookies

1 cup peanut butter
1 cup sugar
1 egg
1 tsp. vanilla

Cream together peanut butter and sugar. Stir in egg and vanilla until well combined. Roll into balls and place on cookie sheet. Flatten slightly with fork.
Bake at 350 for 10 - 12 minutes.

Cookies & Considerations:

The miracle is that these four ingredient, flour-less cookies, actually do work. I don't know how, but then, I don't need to know how all miracles work.

Easy enough to stir by hand, and great for those with gluten allergies.

"Could a greater miracle take place than for us to look through each other's eyes for an instant?"
Henry David Thoreau

Carpe Diem! Seize the Day!

"All of us are walking around with some kind of card we would like to give - some personal expression of joy, creativity, or aliveness that we are hiding under our shirt." So says Alan Cohen, author of The Dragon Doesn't Live Here Anymore.

The recent passing of a friend's father led me to think about Mary.

Mary and I communicated and interacted with each other through the cards and letters we exchanged. She completely surprised me once by enclosing a $20.00 bill for the kids. That twenty dollar bill remains neatly pressed between the folds of the card she'd sent, thanking me for the chocolate and cookies I'd sent.

The remarkable value of her friendship, kindness, faith and hope, magnified itself through that card and $20.00 bill. Although spending it wouldn't detract from the depth of her love, I like knowing it's there. Both the card and the $20.00 bill are reminders of the love she was willing to put out, without fear or expectation.

It would have been easy for Mary to hide that love under her shirt. She was frail and hunched over. Her hands, gnarled from arthritis, composed cards and letters written at a wobbly tilt. From beginning to end, the writing gradually became more of a scrawl, meandering a winding path across the page. Every word she wrote meant more to me because I knew the effort it cost her to write. Every card was a miracle.

One summer, I dreamt I found her wandering in the woods on a crisp fall day. I came upon her on a forest trail tinged with the crispy, dried leaves and grasses of Mother Nature's autumn clutter.

I was surprised to find Mary in the forest, meandering, like her words on the page. Her presence seemed out of place to me.

I tried, that day, in my dream, to take Mary home, afraid she would get lost. Still, she refused to go, declaring that she was already home.

With no other choice, I went on my way, ending my dream and my sleep, in an acute state of awareness.

The next day, worried about her, I went to see Mary. She was fine, but later that year, on a crisp fall day, Mary passed away.

That's when I realized that Mary, who had expressed her joy, creativity and aliveness, so well in her cards to me, was right. I had tried to help her get home, but she was already home. I was the one who was lost.

Sending cards, words of encouragement, sometimes a little gift, shows, with actions and words, how we feel.

We can use cards in the literal sense, meaning with a pen and paper, or as a metaphor for a figurative way to express our feelings when we seize a moment and take the time to show our appreciation to the special people in our lives.

Either way, the message is the same. When we show delight we would normally hide, when we listen to what our hearts are asking us to do, when we open our hearts and give love without fear, when we impart a personal expression of love - we let others know we care.

Carpe diem! Seize the day! Take the time to show someone how much you care.

* * *

For friends named Mary, eating chocolate in heaven or on earth - for friends whose loved ones have passed away - for those of us who, literally and figuratively, give cards - and especially for Linda, who gave me a card with this beautiful message on it. . .

Food for thought:
"The cure for anything is salt water - sweat, tears or the sea."
Isak Dinesen

Express!

Love Letters
Cookies & Considerations
on following page.

Love Letters

Filling:
2 egg whites
1/4 cup sugar
1/2 tsp. cinnamon
3/4 cup ground almonds
1/2 tsp. vanilla
1/4 tsp. almond extract

Dough:
2 cups flour
1/2 tsp. salt
1 cup butter
2 Tbsp. sugar
2 eggs yolks
extra sugar

Beat egg whites till stiff. Beat in sugar and cinnamon. And almonds, vanilla and almond extract. Set aside.

Combine flour and salt. Set aside. Cream butter and sugar. Beat in egg yolks. Gradually add flour mixture. On a floured surface, roll out to 1/4" thickness. Cut into 3" squares. Place 1 tsp. of filling in the center of each square and fold corners diagonally into the center, like an envelope. Place on baking sheet.

Bake at 350 for 18 - 20 minutes. Sprinkle with extra sugar.

Cookies & Considerations:

The other cure for anything is love. These delightful shortbread-like cookie envelopes, are stuffed with love in the form of an almond meringue filling. They're a little fiddley, but they express the joy, creativity and aliveness that we are all walking around with. Give some as an expression of your love.

Honey & Lemon Oatmeal Raisin Walnut Cookies

4 cups rolled oats
3 & 1/2 cups flour
2 tsp. baking soda
2 tsp. salt
1 cup butter
2 & 1/2 cups sugar
4 eggs
2/3 cup honey
grated rind of 1 lemon
2 cups raisins
1 cup walnuts

Combine rolled oats, flour, baking soda and salt. Set aside. Cream butter. Add sugar. Add honey, eggs and lemon rind. Add flour mixture. Add raisins and walnuts. Drop from spoonfuls onto greased baking sheet.
Bake at 350 for 8 - 10 minutes.

Cookies & Considerations:

Comfort foods - a must during times requiring tremendous courage and character development. These cookies are a chewy blend of oatmeal, raisins and walnuts, with the comforting flavors of honey and lemon. (Only chicken noodle soup can be more comforting than the combination of honey and lemon, but it doesn't make a very tasty cookie!)

How to Let Them Go When They're Already Taking the Next Step

A parade always brings tears to my eyes - tears that have nothing to do with the droppings of horses ridden by handsome cowboys and dashing wardens!

Helium-filled balloons traveling their final, lofty flight to the angels; old cars, new cars, small cars, shiny cars; resounding marching bands with bag pipes and cymbals; brass musical instruments in all sorts of twisted shapes and sizes; drums you can feel rumble in your tummy; small children, big dogs, cadets; bicycles, clowns and men in gold-tusked shoes; flying change going one way; candies, bubble gum and balloons going the other. From waving my best royal wave to the visiting monarchy, to greeting the mega-hunk male "Mike From Canmore" - parades are one of my favorite things.

As I began watching my 18th Canada Day Parade in Canmore, I thought back 10 years. In 1989, we had just twinned with our sister city Higashikawa, in Japan; we were discussing whether to rename "Chinaman's Peak"; garbage-loving bears were a pesky problem; cable had 18 channels; housing was a dilemma; and "Batman" and "Dead Poets Society" were held over for three and four weeks respectively, at the Lux.

In 1989 my youngest son, eight months old at the time, earned us both a spot on the front page of the Canmore Leader. His "flag waving frenzy" caught the photographer's eye as we waited, 10 years ago, for his first ever Canada Day parade.

We can't deny it. Our children, more than anything else, give us constant reminders of the passage of time. They also remind us that one day, sooner than we think, the time will come to let go.

As parents, we're obliged to act as if we know what's best for our children. Sometimes it's an act worthy of an Academy Award. Inevitably, as time marches on, we wonder what we could have done differently or not at all and what we didn't do, that we should have.

Whether we need to let go of our children or a painful relationship or circumstance, the lessons can be difficult ones to learn. The process itself stirs up a complex medley of emotions. Feelings of sadness, despair, rejection, fear and doubt are common.

Even so, we can honor the process of growth and change by stepping back and surrendering. Throw your hands in the air, give your head a shake, squeeze out another tear and try something else.

Instead of dictating, plotting and maneuvering chose to find peace by depending on love and faith.

Realize that you were never really in charge anyway.

Ultimately, a higher power is at work. Give it room to work it's magic.

Sometimes that's our best course of action.

* * *

In 1989, I probably wouldn't have given a recipe away.

A few things have changed since then.

When I first started writing my column for the Leader, someone asked me what I was going to do now that I was giving away all my secrets.

There are no secrets. If you believe in abundance, there is no reason for fear, lack and jealousy. All that you let go comes back, many times over.

Food for thought:
"Much that I sought, I could not find; much that I found, I could not bind; much that I bound, I could not free; much that I freed, returned to me."
Lee Wilson Dodd

Let Go!

Chipits® Chewy Milk Chocolate
Cookies & Considerations
on following page.

Chipits® Chewy Milk Chocolate Cookies

1. Beat 2/3 cup (150 ml) melted butter, 2 cups (500 ml) lightly packed brown sugar, 2 eggs, 2 Tbsp. (30 ml) hot water; mix well.
2. Stir in 2 & 2/3 cups (650 ml) all-purpose flour, 1 tsp. (5ml) baking powder, 1 tsp. (5 ml) baking soda, 1/4 tsp. (1 ml) salt.
3. Stir in 1 package (300 g) HERSHEY CHIPITS milk chocolate chips.
4. Drop from small spoon onto ungreased cookie sheet. Bake in 350°F (190°C) oven 10 to 12 minutes.
    Makes 6 dozen cookies.

HERSHEY CHIPITS is a registered trademark. Recipe courtesy of the Hershey Kitchens, and reprinted with permission of Hershey Foods Corporation.
Hershey Foods Corporation

Cookies & Considerations:

Thanks to the Canada Day Committees across Canada and all the volunteers who help put together the Canada Day Parade on every year.

I don't have to be afraid of letting this recipe go, because it was never really mine. You can find the recipe for these easy and yummy cookies, on the back of a bag of my favorite kind of chocolate chips, Hershey Chipits Milk Chocolate Chips.

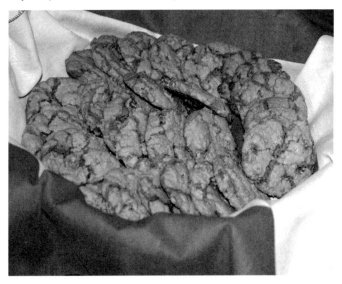

Don's Favorites Or Cecilia's Bestest Cookies
Or Oatmeal Cookies

4 cups flour
4 cups rolled oats
2 tsp. baking soda
2 tsp. baking powder
1 tsp. salt
2 cups butter or margarine
2 cups sugar
2 cups brown sugar
2 tsp. vanilla
4 eggs

optional:
1 cup raisins and/or
1 cup walnuts

cinnamon sugar for rolling

Combine flour, rolled oats, baking soda, baking powder, and salt. Set aside. Cream butter or margarine. Add sugars and beat till light. Add vanilla and eggs. Add flour mixture. Add raisins and/or walnuts (if desired). Roll in cinnamon sugar and drop onto cookie sheet.

Bake at 350 for 10 - 12 minutes or more, depending on size of cookie!

Cookies & Considerations:

I've made these cookies for years, and they remain one of my favorites - especially full of plump, dark raisins and big chunks of walnuts. The recipe went with a column on friendship, and was dedicated to Don, a faithful fan. He called them "The Bestest Cookies". I called them "Don's Favorites". Whatever you call them, you'll call them crispy and chewy, just right to share with a friend and they lend themselves well to making great big cookies - as Don knows! Flatten them slightly before baking.

Makes about 24 - 18" circumference cookies but don't bake them too long or they'll be crunchy, not chewy!

Bittersweet Memories - A Toast to the New Year!

"May all your troubles over the coming year be as short-lived as your New Year's resolutions."

"May you live as long as you want, and never want as long as you live!"

"To our best friends, who know the worst about us but refuse to believe it."

In France, they say, " A votre sante!" In Holland, it's "Geluch!". In Brazil, they cheer "Viva!" In Japan, the toast is "Bonsai!" In Israel, it's "L'Chaim!" And in Ireland the salute to honor in the new year is "Slaintel!"

As the year draws to a close, before reaching for my glass and raising it high to toast good cheer and health, I draw a necessary breath.

As much as I love the holiday season, it's typically very hectic, with not much time for doing the little extras I'd love to have more time for. Knowing it will be hectic, and that there's nothing I can do about it, the next best thing to do is to enjoy it. Be sure to take occasional timeouts for rest, a walk, reading, a game of air hockey, or another feeble, but good hearted attempt at manual dexterity (or the lack thereof) on the Playstation®.

There may not be many quiet moments for a little while, but soon the kids will be back in school and I'll be wishing they were home. The sojourn to relatives will be short and, in time, I'll be wishing that the physical miles between us were not so numerous. Friends and relatives visiting our home will withdraw and the house will seem undecorated and bare. In between, I'll take my deep breaths, enjoy the kids, friends and relatives, and find a quiet moment, whenever I need to reminisce about memories from the past, old and new.

Ornamental memories will soon come down with the tree. The pinecone with feathers - thanks Janet. The withered apple Santa - thanks Carol. The crochet snowflakes - thanks Toots. The brass angel - thanks Oma.

Erma Bombeck called it the memory tree. She also said that, when it comes to un-decorating the tree, if you've had enough people around you to last a lifetime, just say the words, "I'm going to take the Christmas tree down."

In her house, it was a sure way to clear the room, and perhaps the entire house!

As I remove the ornaments, I'll look towards the coming year. I'll wish that, more and more, I have the courage to follow my heart and it's excellent wisdom. No longer do I need to pray for an easy path, only a path that it is clearly marked with messages my heart will recognize. I'll hope that the path is ornamented with courage to help me follow through.

Next year, the path is sure to have many obstacles. I will hope to use them as stepping stones on the path to greater love. A path where I will grow some new memories.

* * *

This message was on a Christmas card, sent to me by a friend, now far away. Along with the rest of us, Susan and her family will bring in the New Year with the creation of new memories and the reminiscence of old. A gift from the past, the beaded Christmas spiders she once gave me hang in my home year-round. They remind me to send along belated Christmas greetings, from the heart.

Food for thought:
"There's a place within our hearts
Where we keep our favorite memories,
The ones that never fail to make us smile -
And when life becomes too hectic
It's such a special feeling
To close our eyes and reminisce a while -
And out of all the memories
Family and friendships,
The ones that are most love-filled moments
That we share at Christmas time -
Those are the dearest memories of all."
Amanda Bradley

Reminisce!

People Puppy Chow
Cookies & Considerations
on following page.

People Puppy Chow

1 - 350 gram box Crispix® cereal
1/2 cup butter
2 cups chocolate chips
1 cup peanut butter
3 cups icing sugar

Empty Crispix® into a large bowl and set aside. Together, melt the butter, chocolate chips and peanut butter. Mix well. Pour over cereal and stir gently till cereal is coated. Add icing sugar and toss till all pieces are well covered and white. Eat! (Not for puppies - only people!)

Cookies & Considerations:

Though these little bite size snacks are not actually a cookie, they are like cookies in that they're a sweet treat that kids love to eat and love to make. For me, they have many memories attached.

The original recipe, which I've long since lost, was printed in a newspaper, years ago. Since then, I've changed it a little, adding more icing sugar, so that each piece of cereal has the appearance of having been individually coated.

I've made them for Birthdays, Valentine's Day, Halloween, Christmas and many times in between. We usually give them out with the recipe attached, but I've been asked for the recipe many times, so here it is once more.

They're an easy (and yummy) way to spend time in the kitchen with your kids before they go back to school. Make some for the New Year or for when you un-decorate the tree. (Maybe someone will stick around to help take the boxes back downstairs.) And there might be some left to take to school for recess, but most likely, they'll probably be only a memory.

Oatmeal Jam Sandwich Cookies

3/4 cup flour
3/4 tsp. baking soda
1/2 tsp. cinnamon
3 cups rolled oats
3/4 cup butter or margarine
1 cup brown sugar
1/2 cup white sugar
1 egg
2 Tbsp. water
2 tsp. vanilla
jam (strawberry, or raspberry, or apricot, or . . . kiwi)

Combine flour, baking soda, cinnamon and oats. Set aside. Cream butter and sugar. Add egg water and vanilla. Cream till light and fluffy. Add flour mixture and mix till blended. Drop dough by spoonfuls onto greased baking sheets. Give them lots of room to spread out, otherwise, you'll have wall to wall cookie! (Not a pretty sight.)

Bake for 10 - 12 minutes or till golden. Cool completely, then spread jam on the flat (bottom) of half the cookies. Put another cookie on top to create a sandwich!

Cookies & Considerations:

That I could inspire a 12 year old boy to read a newspaper column, and then write a poem, amazes me! He inspired me to print this recipe for Oatmeal Jam Sandwich Cookies. Make a whole great big mountain of them because they're easy to make and they smell (and taste) so good! And they really do look like yo-yos!

"Cookies are the greatest thing on earth.
Oatmeal, raisins, and pecans.
Obsession with many cookies.
Kiwi jam in yo-yo cookies
I think cookies are so good I could eat a mountain of them.
Easy to make.
Smell so good."
By Kelsey Hanakowski

Doubts and Uncertainties. . . Welcome to Life

It's certain that, having made countless mistakes through the ages, we aren't certain about the things we used to be certain about. Many of the things we were certain about to begin with have turned out not to be so certain at all. Now, the only thing we are certain about is that we aren't certain about anything - except for the young, who certainly appear to be certain about everything!

Doubts and uncertainties can creep in slowly or suddenly smack you in the face.

They can be subtle and innocent or brutal and insidious.

They can be harmful and detrimental or helpful and beneficial.

Sometimes justified. Sometimes unacceptable.

Sometimes we can see doubt and uncertainty coming. Sometimes we should have seen them coming.

Doubts and uncertainties. . . welcome to life.

When we doubt, it is often because we have seen, felt or been told something that doesn't quite harmonize with what we had planned. Like the proverbial snowball, rolling quickly downhill, we add to our doubts and uncertainties with fear, anger and frustration. Soon, our doubts become a source of distrust, hesitation, questions, floundering, and second guessing. It sometimes becomes difficult to believe that we have a special purpose, when it seems as if things are going against us.

Our general predicament is that the circumstances we find ourselves in are rarely what we think they should be. We try to make do in a situation that seems a far cry from anything we would have chosen to begin with. We don't think we have the strength, wisdom and virtue we need.

However, a change in our attitude, and the way we look at things, can help.

We destroy doubt, by looking at people and situations as personal challenges, another way to learn, and opportunities to understand. Recognizing that things are just as they should be, and just as they need to be, can lead to certainty, assertion, acceptance and faith.

It is our lot as human beings to be all that we can be. When something happens that threatens to hold us back, when someone says or does something that makes us doubt ourselves, realize that, with every situation, we are changing and developing, getting stronger, transforming, and learning a new awareness of something we'd previously not seen and understood.

Our tests and trials are our training ground. If we proceed, it is on beliefs and probabilities, but not certainties. There are few certainties.

We shouldn't worry if we can't be certain of a final outcome. Nor should we let our doubts make us lose, by fearing to even begin. And when we do our best, and still meet with disappointment, humiliation and mortification, perhaps there's another lesson to learn before we can proceed.

Doubts and uncertainties are a part of life. Our goal is to live with uncertainty, without being immobilized by doubt. It starts by embracing a situation with total acceptance. No judgment, no demands, no tantrums. It is certain!

Food for thought:
"The only limit to our realization of tomorrow will be our doubts of today. Let us move forward with strong and active faith."
Franklin Delano Roosevelt

Encourage!

"Hard Tack"
Cookies & Considerations
on following page.

"Hard Tack"

3 & 3/4 cups flour
1 & 1/2 cups butter
3/4 cups sugar
2 tsp. vanilla

Measure flour and set aside. Cream butter and sugar until light and fluffy. Add vanilla. Blend in flour. Press into bottom of 13" X 9" pan and prick all over with a fork (or shape into cookies).

Bake at 350 for 30 - 35 minutes or until golden brown. Cut while still warm.

Cookies & Considerations:

We all need encouragement to keep our doubts and uncertainties at bay. My thanks to Amy, for some kind words of encouragement.

Her dad, Richard, brought me some Mexican vanilla, which was a wonderful surprise, so I made him these shortbread squares. I used to make them years ago and I'm not certain why, but he calls it Hard Tack (not "Heart Attack", which is what Sharon called it).

With loving fondness and a twinkle in his eye, Richard used to say they could stop a bullet - then he'd tell me he was just teasing! I'm certain he was, because since trying this batch, he says, "It's like eating love." Thanks, Richard, I should have put that on the back cover!

It's a firm and tasty shortbread that's made especially tasty with the addition of some Mexican vanilla. (The dough can also be made into cookies. It is certain!)

Cookie Dessert Bowls

2/3 cup flour
1 cup sugar
1/2 cup melted butter
4 egg whites
1 tsp. almond extract
1 tsp. vanilla
4 tsp. water
1/2 to 3/4 cup sliced, toasted almonds

Whisk all ingredients together except almonds, until blended. Drop batter onto greased and floured or parchment lined cookie sheets, using 3 Tbsp. of batter per cookie. Spread into 6 inch circles. Sprinkle with almonds.

Bake at 350 for 8 - 10 minutes, or until edges turn golden brown.

Immediately, lift a cookie with a metal spatula and drape over an upside down measuring cup, shaping it gently and quickly. (Try not to work with more than 4 cookies at a time.)

Serve with ice cream or frozen yogurt or sherbet and fresh fruit or liqueur.

Makes 8 - 12 dessert cups.

Cookies & Considerations:

A great summertime treat - goes well with whatever fruit is in season.

Parchment paper is a big help.

Dear Teacher

Whether we're ready or not (and we rarely are!), Christmas comes, the initial snow of winter falls, and the first day of a new school year arrives.

For many of us, our emotions run high, our tears are precariously perched near the rim and it's hard on our hearts. As parents, we loiter about nervously, searching for our child's name, under yours, on a list. We hope that the two of you will be a perfect match.

Once our children are ensconced, it's hard to leave the school alone, but we do. Admittedly, it is often with trepidation that we entrust our children to your care for another school year. We hope that it is a good year.

That first day quickly passes. We continue our daily delivery. Amongst all of their belongings, the most precious treasures our children bring with them to school, are their delicate spirits and their fragile souls.

Because we know the essence of those treasures, their value, their worth, as well as their need for nourishment, our parental concerns run high. So do our expectations. We hope that you do not think that they are too high.

You see, Teacher, it's true that we need you to teach our children Math and Language Arts. We need you to teach them that $2 + 2 = 4$, and where to put a comma and a period. We need you to teach our children all that is in the school curriculum. We hope that you teach them much more.

We need you to teach our children that they are unique individuals.

Teach them that they are different from every other child you've ever had in your classroom. We hope that you cherish our children, for whoever they may be. Teach them that they have the capacity for great things. Though you may not know what those things are, anymore than we do at any given time. We hope that you feel that our children are worthy of your utmost efforts.

Build their self-esteem, facilitate their growth, and promote the discovery of new skills. Guide them in boosting their abilities. Celebrate their accomplishments. Help them unfold. Support their improvement in all areas, but especially in those that would limit their progress. We hope that if you see a need that has been left unfulfilled, that you will be able to advise how to fill it.

Also, Teacher, please encourage our children to anticipate learning with wonder and excitement. Make their education challenging and stimulating. We want you to care. We hope that you do.

56

Considering all that we have at stake, we hope that you will understand when we become vocal advocates for our children. We want our children to be safe under your guardianship. We hope that they are.

We don't profess to have all the answers. In fact, sometimes we have more questions than answers. Please know that we want only what is best for our children. We hope that is what you want as well.

As teachers, you will be remembered for many years. This year your values and standards will rub off on our children. What and how our children remember, is up to you. We hope that there will be mutual admiration.

We are the parents. Like Christmas and the first snow, we hope that somehow, it all works out, whether, we're ready or not (and we rarely are!).

Take care, love. . .

Food for Thought:
"If you can't hold children in your arms, please hold them in your heart."
Mother Clara Hale

Encourage!

Whole Wheat, Chocolate Peanut Butter Chip
Cookies & Considerations
on following page.

Whole Wheat Chocolate Peanut Butter Chip Cookies

4 & 1/2 cups whole wheat flour
1 & 1/2 cups cocoa
2 tsp. baking powder
2 tsp. baking soda
2 tsp. salt
2 cups butter or margarine
2 cups peanut butter
2 cups sugar
2 cups brown sugar
4 eggs
1 Tbsp. vanilla
1 - 300g pkg. peanut butter chips
extra sugar

Combine flour, cocoa, baking powder, baking soda, and salt. Set aside. Cream butter, peanut butter and sugars. Add eggs and vanilla. Beat well. Add flour mixture and mix well. Add peanut butter chips. Roll into balls and drop in sugar. On cookie sheet, flatten slightly with fork.
Bake at 350 for 12 minutes.

Cookies & Considerations:
The double peanut butter, and chocolate in these cookies should be enough encouragement, but they're wholesome as well. I hope every delectable bite facilitates the nourishment of the heart, body, spirit and soul.
Make some for a recess snack or for your Dear Teacher.

Apricot Amaretto Cookies

1 cup flour
1 tsp. baking soda
1/4 tsp. salt
2 & 3/4 cups rolled oats
1/2 cup sliced almonds
1/2 cup snipped, dried apricots
1 cup butter
1/2 cup sugar
3/4 cup brown sugar
1 egg
1 Tbsp. Amaretto liqueur

Optional: melted chocolate (I use semi-sweet and milk) for drizzling

Combine flour, baking soda, salt and rolled oats. Set aside. Cream butter with sugars. Add egg and Amaretto. Add flour mixture. Add almonds and apricots. Drop onto baking sheet.
Bake at 350 for 10 - 12 minutes or till golden. Drizzle with melted chocolates.

Cookies & Considerations:
A birthday tradition we have in our family is that everyone gets a gift on everyone else's birthday. My gift to you on my birthday is one of my most sought after cookie recipes.
It has been promised for this day, since I began writing a weekly column. As promised, here is my *still* most requested cookie..

Dearest Santa

You probably know this already but I haven't been very perfect this year. When you check your list twice you might see that sometimes I've been naughty - although not nearly as often as I'd like! Sometimes I've been nice - but again, not nearly as often as I'd like. That leaves a lot of gray area, doesn't it, Dear Santa? I'll have to work on that. I am trying my very best, though, so I'm writing early in case I can still get all that I wish for. My Christmas list is long this year, so I'll get right down to it.

This year, for Christmas, I would like you to give me at least a dump truck full of Grace. I would like it to contain ample serenity, elegance, charm and beauty. Kindness is a part of Grace too, so you see, Dear Santa, it would help me show good will and love if I could get some Grace for Christmas.

Mercy and the ability to forgive would also help me know a true sense of Grace in one of its most wonderful forms, so please ensure that I have an abundant supply. Holiness, love and devotion are part of Grace, so I'd like you to include some of that in your gift as well. Also contained in the gift of Grace, I would ask you for invocation, so that I may be capable of offering blessings and thanksgiving for all the wonder in my life.

Success, Dear Santa, is the next gift that I wish for. To know that mastering my accomplishments and achievements will bring me riches and prosperity would be a wonderful present.

Can one ever have enough Knowledge, Dear Santa? I think not, so this year, for Christmas, would you please bring me information, so that I may have enlightenment and wisdom? Please bring me a joy for learning, and if you have some extra comprehension and perception for me, I'm sure I could put it to excellent use. While you're at it, could you throw in some good judgment and insight, so that I am able to discern right from wrong and what is best for me and the fires burning in the deepest embers of my heart?

I think, Dear Santa, that I really need some Strength for Christmas this year. If you can, would you please bring me energy, power, and vigor? Please bring me the capacity to go on. Give me, if you can, the acumen to know how to be effective. Give all that I do the benefit of potency, depth and intensity. With my Strength, could you give me concentration, and a bright and vivid appreciation for newness? Please help me see, with intense clarity and enthusiastic fervor, where all my true Strengths are.

In case I haven't covered it in any of my other wishes, Dear Santa, please let me have my Health. Give me soundness of body and mind, as well as wholeness. Please give me lively well being and fitness. If I could, I'd also like freedom from disease and lack of ailments. Also, could you please give me an extra gift of stamina?

I think that one of the finest gifts I can receive is Happiness, Dear Santa. Please give me cheerful satisfaction in my life. Let me have rapture and euphoria. Please fill my stocking with bliss and contentment and just a little bit of tranquillity. If you can, Dear Santa, I'd like to see that you give me the gift of merriment and joy. Please give me mirth and good cheer, vivacity and delight. Because it's so very precious to me, please, please bless me with the gift of laughter and hilarity, as well as childlike exuberance and gaiety!

My last wish, Dearest Santa, is also one that I consider to be of the highest value. That wish is that you show the world my beauty, so that I may show the world yours.

Thank you in advance, Dear Santa. I know I'm asking for a lot, so you don't have to bring me my gifts all at once. To make it easier on you, I've already started looking for some of the gifts I've wished for. (I think I can find them if I shop locally. Indeed, it's a fact that I've already found some of them, and they came at a wonderful price - a bargain, really!)

Merry Christmas, Dear Santa! Merry Christmas, Everyone!

Food for thought:
"The fragrance of what you give away stays with you."
Earl Allen

Ask!

Melting Moments
Cookies & Considerations
on following page.

Melting Moments

1 & 3/4 cups flour
1 & 3/4 cups cornstarch
1 tsp. baking powder
1 & 3/4 cups butter
1 & 1/4 cups icing sugar

Measure flour, cornstarch and baking powder. Set aside. Cream butter and sugar. Gradually add flour mixture, beating till it forms a ball. Roll dough into small balls and place on greased cookie sheet. Press dough down with cookie press or fork.

Bake at 350 for 20 minutes. Cool completely and ice or put together with raspberry jam or butter icing or . . .

Butter icing:
1/2 cup butter
2 cups icing sugar
2 Tbsp. milk or cream (to spreading consistency)

Whip butter. Add icing sugar and milk or cream.

Cookies & Considerations:

Irene requested these cookies called Melting Moments. Dear Santa, I think she'd make a perfect Mrs. Claus if you're ever looking. Wink! Wink! (I hope you don't think I'm being naughty again because I'm definitely being nice!) On Christmas Eve, we'll leave the usual treats out for you and the reindeer. Maybe I'll leave some more of these cookies out and hope you all have time for a "melting moment".

Shortbread cookie sandwiches with a butter-icing filling. Sounds like a moment to melt for to me.

Coconut Kisses Cookies

9 Tbsp. rice flour
1 & 1/2 cups sugar
1/4 tsp. salt
4 & 1/2 cups coconut
6 egg whites

Optional: 8 ounces (approx.) chocolate for dipping

Combine rice flour, sugar, salt and coconut. Set aside. Whisk egg whites lightly and add dry ingredients. Mix. Drop onto greased cookie sheet, or cookie sheet lined with parchment paper.

Bake at 350 for 12 minutes or till edges and tops turn golden. Cool. If desired, melt chocolate (use semi-sweet or milk, whatever you like most). Dip the bottom of each cookie in the chocolate. Set the cookies on their tummies (upside down) to set. Eat sitting right side up!

Cookies & Considerations:

These gluten-free, light, chewy cookies, with their bottoms dipped in chocolate, are two flavors that compliment one another perfectly.

They're one of my favorites and so easy to make.

Use parchment paper on the baking sheets for an easier clean up.

"A baby is born with a need to be loved - and never outgrows it."
Frank A. Clark

Keeping the Faith - A Letter to Santa

Dear Santa,

Your gifts to me in the past deserve my extended and grateful praise. The grace and mercy you placed beneath my tree were more helpful than I could have imagined. If you had given me nothing more, I would have been content since they saved me so many times.

The strength and knowledge you sent were also beneficial. They continue to be very illuminating at times when I'm sure I need them the most, particularly when I would rather not have to be neither strong nor wise.

You gave me the gift of beauty - not my own physical beauty, but the ability to see the beauty of your world. You have presented me with the aptitude to communicate your beauty to those about me. Thank you for choosing me to be one of your helpers. In showing your beauty, and love, to others, I have received great pleasure.

You see, Santa, your grace and mercy along with the strength and knowledge I've been given have helped me to see that there is a rare beauty in blind belief. With belief, comes the knowledge that I already possess every spiritual blessing possible, and that all of my needs will be met - I will be provided for.

Nonetheless, I do have a few wishes this year. The difference is that, this year, my requests are not only for myself, but also for a people torn apart. It breaks my heart, Santa, to see so many people hold back from offering love and seeing beauty. They choose, instead, to live in anger, fear, hatred, jealousy, greed, gossip, impatience and conceit. Thank you for helping me to see their beauty, even when it tests me to the depths of my beliefs.

With all the Christmas spirit in the air, it seems like a perfect time for a seasonal wish - a year-round, worldwide wish. My heart dreams big dreams, Santa. These are my requests for the year.

We all need peace, hope and joy. I would be remiss if I did not wish for them for the entire world. But that's not my only wish.

I wish for all the world to hear the angels sing. It is an unusual request, I know, but the beauty of faith includes a few angels. I believe.

This year, Santa, to all who request it, bestow my wish that we receive the gift of time to heal our hearts so that they may feel, the gift of clear minds to hear your urgings so that we may follow, the gift of rapture to grow our spirits so that we may encounter harmony and the gift of tenderness to love our souls so that we may uncover our essence.

I have to say, Dear Santa, that although I used to regret that I was given the gift of a sensitive nature, these days, I consider it to be one of my most treasured personal possessions. I value my ability to empathize with others so it is for that reason that I make my wishes primarily for those who cannot see your beauty and for those who live without your love.

I lay my requests before you and wait in hopeful expectation.

Food for thought:
"When his joy invades our lives, it spills over into everything we do and onto everyone we touch."
Charles Swindoll

Wish!

Angel
Cookies & Considerations
on following page.

Angel Cookies

1 - 400 gram pkg. puff pastry, thawed
approximately 1 cup sugar
1 - 9 gram pouch vanilla sugar

Combine sugars and sprinkle the sugar over work surface and roll out half the pastry. Flip dough over and repeat on other side until pastry is about 8 x 10", using more sugar as needed. Cut dough with gingerbread-girl cookie cutters and place on parchment lined cookie sheet. Roll out other half of dough in similar fashion. Cut dough in half. Cut more gingerbread girls out of one half. With the other half, cut 6 thin strips (approx. 1/4" by 2 -3") for each angel - these are the wings! Pinch the strips together in the center and press firmly to underneath of angels. Sprinkle generously with more sugar.

Bake at 400 for 15 - 20 minutes or till dark golden brown and lovely. (Bake the scraps too - they're yummy!)

Cookies & Considerations:

My letters to Santa have become a holiday tradition. Although I know that a prayer to God is much more than a letter to Santa, it's a pretty sneaky way to disguise it.

I have another wish.

I wish to find the owner of this doll. Surely, she must be missed.

We found her while getting our Christmas tree. We picked her up, from where she lay in the snow, and brought her here. I wish for her to be home for Christmas, but if she should remain with me, she will be loved and well cared for.

Santa, if anyone at all knows where she belongs, please have the angels send those people to me.

These angels are heavenly. Puffed up and encrusted with crispy, caramelized sugar, they're easy to make. I believe.

Pistachio Sugar Cookies

3 cups flour
1 tsp. baking powder
1/2 tsp. salt
1 cup butter
2 cups sugar
2 eggs
2 tsp. vanilla
1 cup pistachios
extra sugar for rolling

Combine flour, baking powder, and salt. Set aside. Cream butter and sugar. Beat in eggs and vanilla. Add flour mixture and nuts. Drop by spoonfuls into sugar and roll. Flatten cookies with a fork.

Bake at 350 for 12 minutes or until golden around the edges.

Cookies & Considerations:

Pistachios are such treasures. Encased in their shells, merely eating one requires a certain passionate appreciation. Take some along to the Folk Festival. While you sit and listen to the music, you can shell a cup full or two for these crispy-chewy sugar cookies.

"Memory is a child walking along a seashore. You never can tell what small pebble it will pick up and store away among is treasured things."
Pierce Harris

A Post "Doomsday" Quiz

I put off writing my column as long as I could this week.

I figured that if predictions were correct, and the world did end on Thursday, I might as well not spend my time doing things that wouldn't really matter by next Tuesday.

So, in fervent preparation for the end of the world, on Wednesday I ate my Lindt Pistache Chocolate Bar.

Since it's now Friday, and since the world didn't end - again! - I thought I'd better get busy.

What if it had been the end of the world, though? How would we spend our time if we knew we only had an hour, a day, a week, a month, or a year? What would we do? What would we change - a few things, a lot of things, everything?

In order to help you, I've prepared a Post "Doomsday" Quiz! I'll wait while you get a sharpened HB pencil and some acid-free, lignin-free paper. Please answer the following questions in your head:

If you knew you only had an hour, a day, a week, a month or a year, would you call or write a friend you hadn't heard from in a while?

If time allowed, would you go on a cruise or a trip around the world?

If your stamina allowed, would you climb a mountain?

If your conscious allowed, would you eat all the points off the watermelon wedges?

If your vocal cords allowed, would you crank up the radio, throw open closed doors and sing at the top of your lungs?

Would you go for a walk or stay in bed all day?

Would you leave the lid up and the seat down or both the lid and the seat up or both the lid and the seat down? Would you worry if the toilet paper didn't come under or over?

In the past 200 or more Doomsday predictions, have you ever thought that you should call your Mom and/or Dad?

Would you call an estranged relative or friend and say, "I'm sorry. Can we come to an agreement?"

Would you have cereal for supper? At midnight? In the living room?

Would you watch a "girl movie", soak in the tub, put in too much bubble bath and light more candles?

If you had the inclination, would you go camping? Or fishing?

Would you light the fireplace and snuggle on the couch?

If your sense of humor allowed, would you learn to laugh at yourself?

If your stubbornness allowed, would you let someone else win?

Would you spend less time doing tasks that have no meaning?

Would you spend more time getting to know your children and talking to your partner?

Would you quit your job and learn something new?

Would you chase after a dream?

If courage permitted, would you become the person you want to be?

If you knew you only had an hour, a day, a week, a month, a year, would you express more love and live more from the heart?

If you answered yes to any of the above, give yourself a hug (or see me after the quiz).

The last question is the most difficult one. Please have your sharpened HB pencils and acid-free, lignin-free paper ready.

Answer the following question in your head:

What's stopping you?

Food for thought:

"If you had an hour to live and could make only one phone call - who would you call, what would you say and why are you waiting?"
Stephen Levine

Go!

Double Chocolate Walnut Refrigerator
Cookies & Considerations
on following page.

Double Chocolate Walnut Refrigerator Cookies

2 & 3/4 cups flour
1/2 tsp. baking powder
1/4 tsp. baking soda
1/2 tsp. salt
1/2 tsp. cinnamon
1 cup butter
1 cup sugar
1 cup brown sugar
1 egg
1 tsp. vanilla
4 ounces semi-sweet chocolate, melted and cooled slightly
1 cup semi-sweet chocolate mini chips or chunks
1 cup chopped walnuts

Combine flour, baking powder, baking soda, salt and cinnamon. Set aside. Cream butter or margarine and sugars. Beat in egg, vanilla and melted chocolate. Add flour mixture, chocolate chunks and walnuts. Shape dough into 3 - 8" logs and wrap in waxed paper or plastic wrap. Chill several hours or overnight. Slice into 1/4" slices and place on cookie sheets.
Bake at 350 for 10 - 12 minutes.

Cookies & Considerations:
I made the dough for these scrumptious, crispy refrigerator cookies on Wednesday. Since it keeps for a week refrigerated or 2 months in the freezer, it can be used to quickly bake fresh cookies anytime. Mine was doomed not to last so long - I baked them all on Friday!
What are you waiting for? Go make some!
Taking the time for chilling makes this cookie a lot easier.
Give them extra room to spread.

Almond Biscotti

4 cups flour
1 & 3/4 cups sugar
1/4 tsp. salt
pinch of saffron
1 tsp. baking soda
5 eggs
2 Tbsp. Amaretto
1 cup toasted almonds, ground
1/2 toasted, sliced almonds
1 egg white (for glazing)
extra sugar

Combine flour, sugar, salt, saffron and baking soda in a large bowl. Add eggs and Amaretto and mix thoroughly. Add almonds and knead slightly.

Shape into 4 logs, about 1 & 1/2 inch round. Place on greased and floured cookie sheet. Brush with lightly beaten egg white. Sprinkle with sugar.

Bake at 350 for 20 minutes. Cool slightly and cut diagonally into 1/2" slices. Bake again at 325 for 15 minutes.

Cookies & Considerations:

Saffron's hard to find, but if you can find it, it will make a big difference to this crunchy cookies. The unique taste will have you crunching back for more.

Parchment paper helps with cleanup, as the egg white glaze might stick to the baking sheet.

Communication Gap, a Matter of Perspective, Or. . .?

Most of us, at some time, have been directly involved in circumstances where a point of view or a situation is misinterpreted.

Depending on the perspective of the storyteller, an offered opinion can appear completely different from what we thought, felt, heard or saw. Someone else's perspective can be so distant from our own thinking that we wonder if we were even on the same planet.

Sometimes our misunderstandings are based on quirky communication (or lack thereof). Sometimes they are simply matters of a different perspective and which version of the truth you're willing to honor. And sometimes our misunderstandings are a way for our own judgment and state of being, to mirror back at us.

I believe that we interpret words, actions and events in different ways because we are different. It doesn't make one of us wrong and the other one right - we just see life in a different way. What we see can be based on a wide variety of attributes. Although our uniqueness makes us difficult to label, many have tried.

The study of morphology separates us into body types. The three groups have psychological differences pertaining to action, feeling and mind. Astrology divides us into 12 groups. There's also the Chinese Zodiac, and countless other ways of generalizing and categorizing people, including the way we were raised.

Our upbringing teaches us different values, ideals, and ways of resolving disagreements. As we grow up, we quickly learn that being different sometimes means being laughed at or teased. We feel the need to conform and often learn, at a tender age, to forget that we are supposed to be different.

Judgments, assumptions and lack of acceptance and appreciation of our differences can unintentionally lead to misunderstandings. What seems rational, justified and legitimate, to one, can seem irrational, inappropriate and illogical to someone else.

From school committees to church groups, family businesses to the home or office, we certainly don't always see things in the same light. It's inevitable that our beliefs, personalities and attitudes will conflict. However, when we partake in unwarranted aggression, belligerent gossip, vile criticism, egotistical infighting, heartless name calling, political maneuvering, resentful tirades, and disloyal, underhanded, unethical behavior, only a semblance of the truth remains. Soon, it too is lost in thick mire of false accusations and misinformation where only harm is done and no one benefits.

Our differences make us susceptible to creating our own rendition of the truth. Almost every opinion has some merit. Being tolerant of someone else's opinion, even while we stand firm on ours, allows us to celebrate our differences. Unconditional love and acceptance of people exactly the way they are requires that we recognize that we are different and that we're supposed to be.

Instead of finding fault, and becoming angry and frustrated by the rejection of our viewpoints, we should try to discover what it is about irritations with others that can lead us to better understand ourselves. Perhaps the perceptions we see reflected back to us can teach us something about our own emotions, actions and behavior.

When someone says or does something you don't approve of, give them consideration and thoughtful understanding. Looking beyond our surface displeasure allows us to see the beautiful gifts that are placed before us in our spouses, children, parents, friends, and neighbors.

The next time a communication gap, or a matter of perspective threatens to block your scenic view, take a moment to look at each encounter as if it were a diverse and a challenging experience that could enrich and expand your perspective.

Food for thought:
"And acceptance is the answer to all my problems today. . . I can find no serenity until I accept that person, place, thing, or situation as being exactly the way it is supposed to be at this moment."
Alcoholics Anonymous

Accept!

Hazelnut Biscotti
Cookies & Considerations
on following page.

Hazelnut Biscotti

1 & 2/3 cup flour
1/2 tsp. baking soda
1/2 tsp. cinnamon
1/4 tsp. salt
2 eggs
3/4 cup sugar
2 tsp. rum
1 tsp. vanilla
2/3 cup hazelnuts

Combine flour, soda, cinnamon and salt. Set aside. Whisk together eggs, sugar, rum, and vanilla. Add flour mixture and stir to mix. Add the nuts, incorporating them well. With floured hands, shape the dough into two plump, 12 - 13" long logs.

Bake at 350 for 35 minutes. Remove from oven. Cool at least 15 - 30 minutes. With a serrated or very sharp knife, cut the logs diagonally, into 1/2" thick slices. Stand the sliced Biscotti on a cookie sheet, with enough room between each one to allow for baking.

Bake at 300 for 10 - 15 minutes or until golden.

Cookies & Considerations:

Biscotti are a very easy, very forgiving cookie. You can allow the Biscotti to cool completely before slicing and they'll be much easier to work with.

Whether or not you like this crunchy, meant-to-be-dunked, twice-baked, Italian version of a cookie is a matter of perspective. If you do like Biscotti, this recipe is willing to tolerate whatever differences you'd like to put into it. The nuts can be varied, and fruit or chocolate can be added. Accept the fact that they're easy to make. Look at them as a diverse and challenging experience that could enrich and expand your perspective!

Panforte

1 & 1/2 cups almonds
3/4 cup walnuts
1/3 cup hazelnuts
3/4 cup dried figs
1 Tbsp. cocoa
1/2 tsp. cinnamon
Pinch pepper
Pinch mace
3/4 cup flour
3/4 cup honey
1/2 cup sugar

chocolate for drizzling
icing sugar

Finely chop almond and walnuts and coarsely chop hazelnuts and figs. Combine in a large bowl with cocoa, cinnamon, pepper, mace and flour. Mix well.

Pour honey into saucepan with sugar and heat until sugar is melted. Do not boil. Remove from heat and add to nuts and fruit. Mix well.

Line an 8" or 10" pan with parchment paper and pour batter into pan. Smooth top and bake at 350 for 35 - 40 minutes. Remove from oven and cool in the pan for 10 minutes. Unmold and drizzle with melted chocolates. Cool on a rack for several hours. Sprinkle with icing sugar. To serve, cut in small wedges.

Cookies & Considerations:

This Italian delicacy is a dense, nutty, almost flourless version of a fruitcake. Before you start with the fruitcake jokes, let me tell you that this isn't that. It's a large flat cookie, baked in a cake pan and cut into small, yummy wedges filled with figs and honey. It's been made in Sienna since the Middle Ages, and once you've tried it, you'll know why.

Wrap the Panforte tightly in foil. It should *not* be eaten the same day.

Please, I beg of you, do not make this without lining your pan!

Free Hugs - One Size Fits All!

What needs no batteries, costs absolutely nothing, is not taxable, or noisy, has no breakable parts, is almost always fully returnable, takes up little space, reduces tension, relieves stress, dispels fears, helps fight illness, eases depression, lifts the spirits, brightens the days, does not pollute, does not have to be tested on animals - although they might like it, knows not the discrimination of age, race, religion, size, social class, or sexual persuasion, can be gotten or given anywhere, helps self-esteem and other matters of wellness, is exhilarating and refreshing, has no harmful side effects, no caloric or cholesterol count, is 100% natural, generates good will, makes us feel safe and loved, is extremely personal, yet not intrusive, and really is one-size-fits-all?

Hugs. Hugs are reminders that our willingness to show love is one of the finest opportunities we are given.

Along with hugs, what are walks through the forest, an awareness of nature, a good laugh, a visit with a friend, a hot bath, a dance with a child, a song to sing, a heartfelt letter, a single flower in a vase, a good book to read in front of the fire with a cup of tea, a bird on the feeder, holding hands, a shared meal, a special moment with a family member, a good night kiss, a bedtime story and other little things that happen everyday?

They are reminders that, while we are here, we are to treasure life. A simple way of doing that is to celebrate ordinary pleasures on a daily basis.

We don't always effortlessly remember, but it is helpful to bear in mind that it is our appreciation for the mundane, the ordinary, the simple, the everyday, the precious seemingly insignificant moments, that really do help us, not only get through, but remind us that every day is special. And since we don't know how long we're going to be here, we should appreciate every day with a passionate intensity.

Elizabeth Kubler-Ross said it wonderfully when she said, "It's only when we truly know and understand that we have a limited time on earth - and that we have no way of knowing when our time is up - that we will begin to live each day to the fullest, as if it was the only one we had."

How often do we take for granted that someone (even ourselves) will always be in this world? Of course, we assume that we will have a tomorrow, but in actuality, that may simply not be the case. We never really know.

Imagine giving thanks every morning that you wake up. Now try it.
Imagine offering more kindness, compassion and love. Now try it.
Imagine showing you care, by opening your heart more. Now try it.
Imagine living every single day, as if it might be your last. Now try it.
Imagine giving more hugs. Now try it.

In the very first Chicken Soup for the Soul book there is a story about Lee Shapiro, the hugging judge. He has a bumper sticker on his car that says, "Don't bug me! Hug me!" He knows the power of a hug. I rest my case!

With a no-questions-asked, not-carved-in-stone, fully returnable, can't-live-without-'em, almost-anytime-is-hug-time policy, does anyone need a hug?

Try it!

Food for thought:
"We need 4 hugs a day for survival. We need 8 hugs a day for maintenance. We need 12 hugs a day for growth."
Virginia Satir

Hug!

Hugs & Kisses
Cookies & Considerations
on following page.

Hugs & Kisses

2 & 1/4 cups flour
1 tsp. baking soda
1/2 tsp. salt
1/2 cup butter or margarine
1/2 cup shortening
1/2 cup sugar
1/2 cup brown sugar
1 tsp. vanilla
1 egg
extra sugar
30 - 40 chocolate kisses

Peel the kisses. Eat one and give yourself a hug!
Combine flour, baking soda and salt. Set aside. Cream butter or margarine and shortening. Add sugar and brown sugar, beating till fluffy. Add vanilla and egg; blend well. Mix in flour mixture. Shape dough into balls and roll in sugar.

Place on cookie sheet and bake at 350 for 10 - 12 minutes or until light golden. Immediately top each cookie hug with a kiss, pressing down gently. Let cookies cool completely.

Cookies & Considerations:

These are very special cookies to me. Taste and everything aside, their meaning is one of the most precious.

The recent passing of two well loved members of our community may further serve as a reminder that we don't know how long we're here. Life is for the living, and they lived life well.

Hugs go out to their families and friends, as well as so many others who will have to cope with the void left by the passing of a loved one.

We each deal with grief in our own way. During times of change and emotional trauma may our own beliefs and faith bring us peace within ourselves and, should we need it, may we possess the ability to reach out for help and a hug.

I call these special cookies Hugs & Kisses. A chocolate kiss is enfolded in a one-size-fits-all cookie dough hug. Does anyone need a hug? Try it.

Work fast to get the chocolate kisses in while the cookies are warm.

Almond Butter Cookies

1 & 3/4 cups flour
1 cups butter
1 cup sliced almonds
1/4 cup sugar
2 egg yolks

extra sugar

Place flour and butter in mixer. Beat till fine crumbs form. Add almonds and sugar. Mix in egg yolks and beat till dough forms a ball. To shape, form into small crescents (like mini croissants).

Bake at 350 for 10 - 15 minutes or till light brown. Sprinkle generously with extra sugar.

Cookies & Considerations:

These fragile, buttery cookies will melt in your mouth and they'll use up some of those egg yolks that hang around after making macaroons, meringues and angel food cake.

"When I stand before God at the end of my life, I would hope that I would not have a single bit of talent left and could say, 'I used everything you gave me.'"
Erma Bombeck

Four Little Words

Dear Mom,

Another Mother's Day has come and gone. Although it's a very special day, meant to honor another common bond we all share - Moms - somehow, it's the normal days that have me appreciating you the most. In many an unspoken moment, you sneak into my thoughts - a gentle reminder of how much I admire you, cherish you, and treasure you. If we were French, Mom, I'd say, "Je t'aime, Maman".

I extend my belated greetings in an effort to declare, in words, the sentiments in my heart. In Italian, my words would be, "Ti voglio bene, Mamma".

The stories I've read, the snacks I've made, the toys I've picked up, the clothes I've washed, the cakes I've baked - they don't amount to much, compared to all that you've done for me over the years. In Spanish, you'd hear me say, "Te amo, Mama".

Through it all, I often wonder what sort of memories I'm creating for my own children. I hope that there will be a great many good ones. If our nationality were Polish, I would proclaim, "Kocham cie, Mamo".

I think of the challenges I have put to you over the years and I am grateful that I never had to ask you to forgive me. You always just did. Unconditionally. If Russian was our first language, I might say "Ya lyublyu, Mamu".

Thank you for always wanting the best for me, even when I couldn't see it for myself. If Swahili were our native tongue, "Nakupenda, Mama", would be what I'd say.

Thank you for always doing the best you could with whatever life threw at you and our family. Thank you for protecting me, nurturing me, loving me, worrying about me, teaching me and guiding me. In German, my devotion could be expressed by uttering, "Ich liebe dich, Mutti".

Thank you for hugging me back. Thank you for keeping me. Thank you for letting me go. In Portuguese, Mom, I'd say to you, "Amo-te, Mae".

Thank you for your advice (even when I didn't want it)! Thank you for letting me value you for who you are - real and lovely and good. Thank you for loving my own children. If I knew Hebrew, I might say, "Ani ohevet ohtach,

Ima".

I think of the care I give my children, my partner, and my friends, acquaintances, colleges. In part at least, I see a reflection of your assurance, nurturing, and fierce love. In Arabic, "Ana ahab, Waladatuka" would be the words I'd use.

As I write this, a deep, yearning need to express my love and gratitude for all that you have done for me, and continue to do, is palpable. In Japanese I'd say, "Okasan arigato".

Mom, you make me proud to be a daughter, a mother, a woman.

Even in a demanding life, there is a moment to shout from the mountaintops, because I can't leave these words unsaid. Just four little words, Mom. In any language, their importance should not be diminished, taken for granted, or presumed.

Today and everyday, "I love you, Mom."

Food for thought:
"The love we give away is the only love we keep."
Elbert Hubbard

Express!

Alphabet
Cookies & Considerations
on following page.

Alphabet Cookies

2 & 1/4 cups flour
1/4 tsp. salt
1 cup butter
1 cup icing sugar
1 tsp. vanilla
3 egg yolks, lightly beaten

Combine flour and salt. Set aside. Cream butter and add icing sugar. Add vanilla and 3 egg yolks. Slowly add flour mixture. Blend thoroughly. Chill dough slightly. Shape and roll dough into letters. Place on greased cookies sheet.

Bake at 350 for 12 - 15 minutes or till golden.

Cookies & Considerations:

When I brought these cookies in to be photographed for the paper, I proudly laid them out on the table and waited excitedly for Carol to photograph them. Instead, she looked at me questioningly and read out what I had so carefully written out . It said "I You Love"!

Please, take extreme care when using these shortbread-like cookies to spell out your words of love.

Banana Cookies

3 cups flour
1 & 1/2 tsp. baking soda
1/2 tsp. salt
1/2 cup shortening
1/2 cup butter
1 cup sugar
2 eggs
1 cup mashed banana
1/2 cup cream
1 tsp. vanilla
1 tsp. vinegar
1 cup nuts
1 cup chocolate chips

Combine flour, baking soda and salt. Set aside. Cream together shortening and butter. Add sugar, eggs, bananas, vanilla, cream and vinegar. Beat till light. Add flour mixture. Add nuts and chocolate chips. Chill for 1 hour. Drop onto greased or parchment lined baking sheets.
Bake at 350 for 12 - 15 minutes.

Cookies & Considerations:
Make a large, soft cookie that will use up those overripe bananas. Not too sweet - the people I gave some to ate them for breakfast and loved them!

"When you give away a little piece of your heart, you're giving away the only thing you can give away, which, after you do, you got more left than you had before you gave some of it away."
Don Hutson

Dad? Have You Got Time To Play . . . Today?

My dad is not a man of many words. Nonetheless, as Father's Day draws near, I'm reminded of something he once said to me. "I worked hard all my life and I don't know if it was worth it."

As his daughter, the words, and the depth of feeling behind them, made me sad. Maybe my dad had let too many important moments slip away until it was too late. Sure, he did the best he could at the time, but he was busy and burdened with the pressures to earn a buck and look after our home. Now retired, he has time to play, but his children have all grown and moved on.

As parents, we all have a lot resting on our shoulders. We know our children are important, but sometimes we're so busy trying to make a living that we forget to make a life.

Martin Luther King, Jr. said, "We are prone to judge success by the index of our salaries or the size of our automobiles rather than by the quality of our service and relationship to mankind."

We get so caught up with meetings and appointments, deadlines and to-do lists, the clutter and fragments of our daily duties, that we forget to see the magnificent wonders and simple enchantments that accompany our children. (Often, even when we do focus on our children, it is with a false sense of importance, placed on the things that won't matter in a week, a month, a year and five years.)

Every time we're not there for our children, is lost time. If we're missing moments with our children out of a misplaced sense of duty, it may be time to re-evaluate.

Our children can help us do that. They bring us many messages. Amongst them are the messages of balance and perspective for each new day.

There are many messages we bring our children. One of the most valuable, is the gift of our presence. By taking the time to enjoy their lives - even if it's only for a few minutes each day - we make them our priority.

Renew the magic with a message of love. But make sure the message you send, gets through. Start with "I love you . . ."

Say it with charisma. Say it with your spirit. Say it with love.

Let the love come, not only from what you do, but from who you are.

Make time to play.

Food for thought:
*"Have you seen anywhere, a dear boy and a girl,
and their small winsome brother of four?
It was only today that barefoot and brown they
played by my kitchen door.
It was only today or . . .
maybe a year . . .
it couldn't be twenty I know . . .
that laughing and singing they called me to play.*

*But I was too busy to go . . .
too busy with finance and home work to play . . .
and now they've grown up and they've wandered away.*

*Someday I know they must stop and look back . . .
and wish they were children again . . .
I'd run out my kitchen door . . .
for there's never a chore that could keep me away*

*. . . could I just hear my children call me to play.
Where are my children?
I've got time . . .
today."*
Anonymous

Play!

"Dad's"
Cookies & Considerations
on following page.

"Dad's" Cookies

3 cups flour
2 tsp. baking powder
2 tsp. baking soda
2 tsp. salt
1/2 cup shortening
1/2 cup butter
2 cups sugar
2 cups brown sugar
4 eggs
2 tsp. vanilla
4 cups rolled oats
4 cups coconut

Combine flour, baking powder, baking soda and salt. Set aside. Blend together shortening, butter, sugar and brown sugar. Add eggs and vanilla. Blend in flour mixture. Add rolled oats and coconut. Roll into balls and drop onto lightly greased baking sheets.

Bake at 350 for 12 - 15 minutes or until golden.

Cookies & Considerations:

These crispy, crunchy, coconut and oatmeal cookies are just right any time, but especially good to share with Dad this Father's Day weekend.

Ask Dad if he's got time to play today.

Chocolate Nut Slice

1 ounce finely grated white chocolate
11 ounces melted semisweet chocolate
3/4 cup condensed milk
1/2 cup pistachio nuts
1/2 cup pecans
1 Tbsp. brandy

Line a 4 inch x 13 inch pan with foil. Sprinkle bottom with white chocolate. Combine remaining ingredients, mixing well. Spread evenly in pan. Cover and refrigerate for several hours or overnight. Keep refrigerated until ready to slice and serve.

Cookies & Considerations:
This is not a traditional cookie, but it's so tasty and easy. You'll impress everyone with how much time it looks like you spent making it. Only you will know that the part that took the longest, was shelling the pistachios!

Will keep refrigerated for 1 week. Do not freeze.

Happy and Sad at the Same Time - With Zero Minutes Left

"We have zero minutes left!", he shouted into the wind.

The young boy and his slightly older brother whizzed past me on their mountain bikes, their shortish legs straining to make up time on their largish bikes. Skateboards strapped to back packs, strapped to shoulders, they were happy from their play, but sad that they had "zero minutes left".

How true, I thought. The news, still in the media, about the violence in schools, reminds us all that we have zero minutes left.

Zero minutes to learn what to do.

Zero minutes to teach it.

Zero minutes left for blame.

Zero minutes left to hide.

Across the continent, countless news items continue, sadly, to dominate the news. It's true that some prefer not knowing, but hoping the issue will disappear won't make it happen.

Anyway, isn't it finally time that we lift the blanket of silence? Isn't it time to acknowledge that a problem exists and it's a problem that belongs to all of us? Isn't it time to stop casually dismissing bullying as another phase of adolescence?

It's not a secret, it's not a phase, it's not new, and it's not acceptable.

Somehow, somewhere along the way, mean-spirited and nasty behavior became a permissible part of puberty. Sadly, most of us have, at one time or other, been abused. Bullying is not restricted to physical violence. Abuse can be verbal or mental, as well as physical. Bullies are not always children and, sadly, as we have seen, what arises from bullying and violence, is more bullying and violence.

Two weeks ago, I was struck, once again, by the violence in schools. This time in a small B. C. community (pop. 2000).

The story is sadly familiar. A 15 year old student made threats to return to school to shoot 10 students and a teacher, after being suspended from school the previous day.

The difference for me, this time, was, that this was the community I'd grown up in. This time, it was the school I'd gone to, before I graduated.

This time, it was the same grade that one of my children would be going to right now, had we stayed.

This youth, like so many of the others, had been bullied. He had been ridiculed, tormented, and made to feel like an outcast. He also had a history of aggressive behavior and suspensions. And then, he'd uttered threats at school.

In light of all that has transpired in the very recent past, we can't afford not to take all threats seriously. So, when a frightened girl told her mother, who then informed the RCMP, the RCMP quickly initiated an investigation, arresting the youth and seizing, from his home, the list of names, 6 knives and 24 guns (6 handguns and 18 long barreled firearms).

The fact that the firearms were properly stored and lawfully owned, by the father, who is a gun collector, does little to ease the mind. Even the RCMP admitted that the weapons were "potentially accessible". The investigation continues, with the youth charged with two counts of uttering threats, to which he has pleaded guilty.

By some measures it might be considered a happy ending; after all, the young man was stopped before he could make good on his threats. At the same time, it's pretty sad that it's come to this.

We have zero minutes left to deal with the issues of harassment, bullying and violence in our schools.

We have zero minutes left to start communicating with, and understanding, each other.

We have zero minutes left to stop the violence and somehow find our way back to peace and love.

Food for thought:
"Abuse is the weapon of the vulgar"
Samuel Griswold Goodrich

Respond!

M&M's® Homestyle Oatmeal
Cookies & Considerations
on following page.

M&M's® Homestyle Oatmeal Cookies

1 cup butter
1 & 1/2 cups brown sugar
1 egg
1 & 1/2 tsp. vanilla
2 1/2 cups rolled oats
1 & 1/4 cups flour
1 cup **M&M's®** Mini Baking Bits
1/4 cup coconut
1 tsp. baking soda
1/2 tsp. salt

Cream together butter and brown sugar. Add egg and vanilla; mix to combine. Blend in remaining ingredients and mix well. Drop dough by rounded teaspoonfuls onto an ungreased cookie sheet.
Bake at 350 for 8 - 10 minutes or until golden brown.

Cookies & Considerations:

At grad ceremonies all around the world, there will be parents attending who are happy, parents who are sad, and parents who are happy and sad at the same time.

And just when you think they don't need you anymore, and you have zero minutes left to be a parent, they come and surprise you with a hug, a kiss, and an "I love you".

Children of all ages love **M&M's®** candies and they will love these cookies, which I'm pleased to say that Effem Inc. has given me permission to print. Their excellent recipe appears on the back of bags of **M&M's®** Mini Baking Bits.

"M&M's" is a registered trademark of Effem Inc.
© Effem Inc.

Lollipop Cookies

6 cups flour
4 tsp. baking powder
1 tsp. salt
2 cups butter or margarine
2 cups sugar
1 cup brown sugar
4 eggs
1 tsp. vanilla
wooden popsicle sticks

Icing:
1 cup butter
6 cups icing sugar
1/4 cup cream

Combine flour, baking powder and salt. Set aside. Cream butter and sugars. Add eggs and vanilla. Mix well. Add flour mixture. Chill dough for 1 hour. Divide dough in half. On lightly floured surface, roll out half the dough to 1/4" thickness. Use a cookie cutter or glass to cut out dough. Place on greased cookie sheet. Place a wooden popsicle stick on the cookie and press down slightly. Place another cookie on top and press gently to sandwich the stick.

Bake at 350 for 10 - 13 minutes or till done, depending on size of cookies. Cool. Meanwhile, cream butter. Gradually add icing sugar and cream, mixing until smooth. Add food coloring, if desired and frost. Decorate with Halloween candies and other decorations.

Cookies & Considerations:
Out of this batch, I made 27-3 inch lollipop cookies. They make wonderful surprise treats also.

(Happy?) Halloween History 101

In Rome, the festival of Pomona began as a celebration of the harvest. The festival, named after the lovely, enchanting goddess of fruits and gardens, used to roast nuts and apples in big bonfires. It was done as a symbol of the fruits stored away for the winter. It was also thought that during the festival, witches and ghosts were on a rambling prowl and straggling traipse through the villages.

The Celtic festival of Samhaim, in the British Isles, also lit bonfires. The Druids, priests and wizards of ancient Britain, Ireland and Gaul, believed that on October 31st, the dead arose from their graves to roam and tour their old homes. The bonfires were lit to prevent lost souls from destroying property. Just in case that didn't work, plan B was to have the frightened villagers offer fruit and nuts to the wandering spirits. Young people carved lanterns from turnips, disguised themselves in masks and strolled the villages.

What originally began as a celebration of autumn festivals, is the history of how the supernatural and physical world met on a night when it was thought that magical spells could be cast more easily and that humans were more susceptible to the power and influence of the unseen. It is also how Halloween and Trick or Treating began!

As with most holidays, customs and traditions have been gathered all through the ages. For Halloween, we also introduce the belief in superstitions.

In ancient times, people relied on superstitions to keep themselves safe from things they did not comprehend. The origin of some of our most choice superstitions is interesting.

In primitive times, black cats were thought to be companions to witches. Supposedly, after seven years, the cats turned into witches or devils. Yikes!

Knocking twice on wood came about when trees were thought to be the homes of the Gods. A person would ask to be granted a wish. One knock was for the wish and the other knock was to give thanks. Knock, knock, anyone home?

Supposedly, seven years of bad luck came from breaking a mirror. The belief was that your reflection was your soul, and in breaking your image, your soul became damaged. Oh, dear!

Today, we avoid walking under ladders out of common sense, but in the Middle Ages it was held that the ladder, which formed a triangle with the floor and wall, was considered a symbol of life. To walk through the triangle meant that you were tempting the fates with your life. My goodness!

How did Friday the 13th, become so scary? Put these all together to spell what, in ancient times, people held to be the most unlucky day in the calendar: There were 13 people at the last supper, Judas was the 13th guest, and Christ died on . . . you guessed it, Friday the 13th!

Food for thought:
"Fear grows in darkness; if you think there's a bogeyman around, turn on the light."
Dorothy Thompson

Influence!

Pastel
Cookies & Considerations
on following page.

Pastel Cookies

3 & 1/4 cups flour
1 tsp. baking powder
1/2 tsp. salt
1 cup butter, margarine or shortening
1 cup sugar
2 egg yolks
1 tsp. vanilla
6 Tbsp. milk
food coloring

Combine flour, baking powder and salt. Set aside. Cream butter with sugar. Beat in egg yolks, milk and vanilla. Blend well. Add flour mixture and blend well. Chill for 1 - 2 hours. To make pumpkins, color about 1/8 of the dough green for the stems and leaves. Color the remaining dough orange and roll out to 1/4" thick. Using a pumpkin cookie cutter or a circle, cut out dough. Place on cookie sheet. With green dough, roll out or form stems for the pumpkin. Add chocolate chip, raisin, nut and candy faces.

Bake at 350 for 10 - 12 minutes.

Cookies & Considerations:

When we go trick or treating, we like to take some home made treats to give to friends, neighbors and the bogeyman, if we see him. Maybe I'll scare up some of these beautifully colored cookies for our Halloween tradition. I'll color them orange and green and shape them into pumpkins, and you can too. Or give in to the unseen power and influence of your own imagination and see what you come up with.

Sour Cream Drops

1 & 2/3 cup flour
1 tsp. baking powder
1/4 tsp. baking soda
1/4 tsp. mace
1/2 cup butter
1 cup sugar
1/2 cup sour cream

Combine flour, baking powder, baking soda and mace. Set aside. Cream together butter and sugar. Add sour cream. Blend in flour mixture. Drop dough onto baking sheets.
Bake at 350 for 12 minutes or until lightly browned.

Cookies & Considerations:
An easy sugar cookie with the tangy twist of sour cream and the spicy zing of mace.

"We look forward to the time when the power of love will replace the love of power. Then will our world know the blessing of peace."
William Ewart Gladstone

God Don't Make Junk

I just got my new glasses. Before that, I was wearing my old broken ones.

For three weeks I walked around with a glob of silver solder above my right eye. At first, it was a small glob, but the small globs didn't hold and had to be repaired five more times, until. . . the last time!

The last time my glasses broke, we were visiting my Mom & Dad for Easter. My glasses repairman set about his duties, once again.

He'd brought along his soldering stuff, but had left his own reading binoculars at home. The result was a five mile wide, sorta round, glob of silver solder, above the left side of my right eye.

It was visible clear across town on a night as dark as Halloween.

Talking to a friend on the phone, I asked, "Can you see it?"

"No, I can't see it," she said.

I suspect she was just being nice. It was big! But it held - thanks to my glasses repair man.

Now, with my crystal clear, no silver solder, brand new eye gear, I can see things much clearer and realize that some things aren't always the way they seem, especially the way we perceive ourselves

We perceive our own images with the harshest criticism and judgment. We seem willing to point out our imperfections, nit-picking about every part of ourselves that doesn't seem to quite measure up.

We think our nose could be smaller, our thighs could be thinner, our tummies could be tighter; our feet prettier, our bosoms higher, our vision 20/20. We could be taller/shorter, more attractive; our voices could be higher/lower. Even our laughter and our curly/straight hair could be perfected. Don't even get me started on cellulite! We could have a better, more wrinkle-free, complexion, less chins, more grace. . . we could go on for hours, and sometimes we do. We dissect everything about ourselves. Never mind that others might think they're treasures. To us, they seem like junk.

Well, God don't make junk.

Our bodies are vessels. We each get one, and only one - whether we like it or not.

Because we often think of ourselves in terms of how we appear, our self-esteem can be crushed if a part of our physical appearance, that we identify ourselves with, changes or isn't what we'd like.

Just like the extra weight on our hips, our self-esteem comes and goes. For many, it will be a life long battle. But, it doesn't have to be. We can learn to make the most of what we have.

Don't war with your thighs (or whatever it is for you). Make peace with them. They're yours and they're the only ones you get. You might as well like them, because wherever you go, there they are.

Love, accept, and respect your body. Treat it like a valuable treasure. It is the greatest piece of equipment you will ever know. Honor its unique needs by listening to it. It will tell you want it needs, if you will listen.

Our bodies are here to teach us that the core of who we are is our spiritual essence. Let your inner beauty be the real source of worthiness.

Sometimes things aren't the way they seem. Sometimes things are exactly the way they seem. Beautiful and perfect in every way. And coming in clearer every day.

Food for thought:
"Your body is your vehicle for life. As long as you are here, live in it. Love, honor, respect and cherish it, treat it well, and it will serve you in kind."
Suzy Prudden

Treasure!

Low Fat Mocha Oatmeal
Cookies & Considerations
on following page.

Low Fat Mocha Oatmeal Cookies

2 cup flour
1 cup cocoa
2 cup rolled oats
1 cup bran
1 tsp. baking powder
1 tsp. baking soda
1/2 tsp. salt
1/2 cup oil
1 cup brown sugar
1 cup sugar
2 large eggs
2 tsp. instant coffee granules
2 tsp. water
1/2 cup coffee yogurt
2 tsp. vanilla

Combine flour, cocoa, rolled oats, bran, baking powder, baking soda, and salt. Set aside. In a mixing bowl, beat oil, brown sugar, sugar and eggs until smooth. Combine coffee powder and water till coffee is dissolved. Add to mixer, along with yogurt and vanilla. Blend in dry ingredients until well combined. Let sit for 10 minutes, while liquid is absorbed. Drop onto lightly greased or parchment lined baking sheets.
Bake at 350 for 8 - 10 minutes or till puffy.

Cookies & Considerations:

Okay, so maybe the glob of solder wasn't really as big as it seemed. . .but it was big!

These moist and chewy, cake-like, cookies seem to be high in fat, but things are not always the way they seem. Clearly, they're low in fat and high in fiber, and the rich brownie-like taste will satisfy your cravings on the days when you're trying to cut down on fat but still want/need chocolate. They're not junk, they're treasures.

Chocolate Chip Refrigerator Cookies

2 & 1/2 cups flour
1 tsp. baking soda
1 tsp. salt
1 cup butter
3/4 cup sugar
3/4 cup brown sugar
1 tsp. vanilla
2 eggs
1 - 12 oz. (300 gram) pkg. milk chocolate chips
1 cup walnuts, chopped

Combine flour, baking soda and salt. Set aside. Beat butter and sugars until creamy. Add vanilla and eggs. Gradually, beat in flour mixture. Stir in chocolate chips and walnuts. Divide dough in half. Chill for half and hour. Shape each half into a 15-inch log and wrap in waxed paper. Chill at least 1 hour. Cut into 1/2 inch slices.

Bake at 350 for 10 - 12 minutes.

Cookies & Considerations:

Chop the walnuts a bit if you want the slicing to go smoother.

Lob off a generous chunk for each cookie, but give them room to spread.

Gifts of Nature at Springtime

One of the most beautiful things I've seen today, is something I see every time we go to Calgary, and then again on the way home.

The panoramic view is picturesque. Snow-capped mountains in the distance, gently rolling hills and farmland in the foreground. It is breathtaking.

Each time that artistic scene reaches me, I feel a renewed sense of awe. I wonder why it seems to be such a mystical experience, and delight in the fact that I don't know. I only know that I enjoy that it moves me.

The landscape seems to be preparing for a languid awakening at spring's quietly murmured beckoning. Winter's long slumber will gradually make way for blossoms and new growth. Before long, dazzling sunlight and brilliant blue skies will help turn the earth green. The reward for our patience will be spring's apparent beauty - a gift from the universe.

There is so much to see and do, that we often neglect to observe the unwrapped gifts and free surprises that nature and creation have to offer. Who has time to pay attention? Life's frantic pace regularly keeps us racing from one emergency to the next.

The world is studded and strewn with visions, cast about by a generous hand. Does anyone notice the blade or two of green grass, amongst many brown blades, the first wild flower burgeoning through a crack in the rigid soil, the enchantment of rocks, their geometric shapes an amazing beauty we obliviously trample? Who sees the rainbows in their primary colors, moving waters that ripple and sparkle, fluffy pussy willows, green leaves waiting to explode out of a branch and creatures of all sorts, emerging from their hiding places?

Nature's spring visions create an invigorating collage of magical beauty. Our minds must be consciously open to the wonders hidden just beyond our confined views. Nature is full of dimensions, depths, and textures, but they can only be observed if we are attentive and appreciative.

If we look for incredible miracles in nature, and if it is our intention to be awed by the preciousness we see, then ordinary things take on whole new meanings. We can train ourselves to look for the extraordinary in the ordinary. We can see harmony in our world, perfection in the universe, and extraordinary beauty in nature.

We see, in life, what we want to see. Search for ugliness, and you will find it. Look for beauty in life and that is where you will find it.

For those who are aware, there is no end to the surprising beauty they are privileged to see. There is no beauty too insignificant to notice and no detail too frivolous to love. There is no observation that lacks a quality of vivid intimacy about it.

We live together in this world, sharing whatever beauty we randomly choose to see. We are all, as adults, and as children, capable of experiencing the beauty of nature. Cherishing a place or vision can transform us, not from necessity, but from love.

And an act of love is a powerful act.

Food for thought:
"Wake up with a smile and go after life. . . . Live it, enjoy it, taste it, smell it, feel it."
Joe Knapp

Double Chocolate Macadamia
Cookies & Considerations
on following page.

Double Chocolate Macadamia Cookies

4 & 1/2 cups flour
1 cup cocoa powder
2 tsp. baking soda
2 tsp. salt
2 cups butter
1 & 1/2 cups white sugar
1 & 1/2 cups brown sugar
2 tsp. vanilla
4 eggs
2 cups white chocolate chips or chunks
1 & 1/2 cups macadamia nuts

Combine flour, cocoa powder, baking soda, and salt. Set aside. Cream butter and sugars. Add vanilla and eggs, beating till creamy. Gradually add flour mixture. Stir in chocolate and walnuts. Drop onto cookie sheets.

Bake at 350 for 9 - 11 minutes or till done.

Cookies & Considerations:
These cookies are a delight for the senses. Enjoy them, taste them, smell them and feel them.

"Peace is seeing a sunset and knowing whom to thank."
Source Unknown

Chocolate Almond Sugar Cookies

4 cups flour
1/2 cup cocoa
2 tsp. baking powder
1 & 1/3 cups butter
1 & 1/2 cups sugar
2 eggs
3 Tbsp. Amaretto
2 tsp. vanilla
1 cup semisweet chocolate chips
1 cup sliced almonds

Combine flour, cocoa and baking powder. Set aside. Cream butter. Add sugar. Beat in eggs, liqueur and vanilla. Add flour mixture, chocolate and nuts. Drop by rounded spoonfuls onto cookie sheets. Flatten each cookie with the bottom of a glass dipped in sugar.
Bake at 350 for 10 - 12 minutes or till firm.

Cookies & Considerations:
A crunchy, nutty cookie.
Liqueur may be substituted with other liqueurs or with milk.

Getting Through the Tough Stuff - It's a Losing Battle!

I was hemming a couple of pair of pants last night when the sewing machine stalled. It whined and chugged, and as it started up again, the needle butted heads with the plate below and snapped the thread into thin, raggedy strands. Tough stuff, I thought!

And how like the majority of us.

We stall, we whine, we chug, we butt our heads and we snap, trying to get through the tough stuff - particularly when it involves significant change.

Change, of any kind, is one of the toughest things we face in our lives. Some of the most meaningful changes occur when we change ourselves, especially when we put an end to a self-destructive habit.

Whether we're addicted to alcohol, drugs, gambling, sex, money, power or food, giving up our vices can be tough stuff.

The only visible vice is the one regarding food.

We are a nation of people besieged, not only with eating disorders like anorexia, body hatred, bulimia, compulsive overeating and chronic over-exercising, but one that is beleaguered with obesity.

For some, food is like a wonder drug. As a mood altering substance, we medicate and comfort ourselves with food. We escape through it, indulge in it, become distracted over it and comfort ourselves with it. For some, food is more than a healthy way to nourish our bodies, it is a tranquilizer, used to the hide pain, joy, hurt, boredom, anxiety, fear, frustration, stress and our feelings.

In a society where our physical appearance is more important than anything that might be on the inside, bars, gums, candies, shakes and prepackaged foods are just some of the products claiming the categorical resolution to all our struggles. The weight loss industry is shaped by more than food, though.

Pills and drugs, vitamins and minerals, both natural and manmade, also assure us of certain success. There are scales and supplements and products advocating that they burn fat. From meal planners, calorie counters, and appetite managers to fat meters, tummy staplers, fat suckers and fad diets, weight loss is big business. And we try it all.

As we stall, whine, chug, butt our heads, and snap, through the tough stuff of another failed diet, we should consider embracing another approach.

Whole person care.

Whole person care is about connecting the body, the mind, and the spirit. It is about transforming an insatiable hunger, which we interpret as physical, to that which it may truly be - a hunger for psychological and spiritual fulfillment.

It's about understanding that no food is forbidden once we devalue the power it has to satisfy a hunger that is not physical. By focusing on our love for a higher power, we can fill ourselves up on a different kind of nourishment - a sustenance that focuses on the fullness in our hearts. A sustenance that is not based on limiting, abstaining and starvation will give credence to a life lived in health and with fullness, richness, joy and love.

When we take the importance that we place on food, and apply it to the dedication and devotion of a God who wants us to be our most magnificent, we change our attitudes and we empower ourselves. Whatever our vices, we can transform our lives. With acceptance, courage and understanding we will see that, eventually, change is a heavenly blessing.

A diet that's not a diet, based, not on food and gluttony, but on enjoyment, integrity, ingenuity, hope, inspiration, motivation and love. No will power, no cravings, no scales, no bad foods or good foods, no counting calories, no menu plan, no magic pills or interesting potions and no uncontrollable hunger.

Think it can't be done? Watch me.

Food for thought:
"Seek not outside yourself, heaven is within."
Mary Lou Cook

Hunger!

Pistachio & Apricot Biscotti
Cookies & Considerations
on following page.

Pistachio & Apricot Biscotti

2 & 1/4 cups flour
1 & 1/4 cups sugar
2 Tbsp. cornmeal
1/2 cup blue cornmeal *
1 & 1/2 tsp. baking powder
1/2 tsp. salt
1 tsp. ground anise
1/2 cup pistachios
1/2 cup slivered dried apricots
grated rind of 1 lemon
1/2 cup butter
3 eggs
1 tsp. anisette flavoring
(*available in the bulk food department or substitute yellow cornmeal)

In a mixer bowl, combine flour, sugar, cornmeal, blue cornmeal, baking powder, salt, ground anise, pistachios, apricots and lemon rind. Add butter and mix until mixture resembles coarse crumbs. Add eggs and anisette flavoring. Dough will be sticky. With floured hands, form dough into logs about 2" wide by 1" thick and 12" long.

Bake at 350 for 30 minutes. Cool. Slice diagonally into 1/4" slices. Bake again for 8 minutes, allowing air to circulate between.

Cookies & Considerations:

Some people think Biscotti are a tough cookie to make. While they are sometimes tough to eat, they're actually fun & easy to make. These ones are not so tough to eat and they're full of a wonderful assortment of flavors and aromas. Maybe you could try just one, to satisfy a physical hunger.

Bird's Nests

3 & 1/2 cups flour
1/2 cup cocoa
2 tsp. baking soda
1 tsp. salt
1 cup shortening
1 cup butter
1 cup sugar
1 cup brown sugar
2 tsp. vanilla
2 egg
extra sugar for rolling
candy coated chocolate Easter eggs

Combine flour, cocoa, baking soda and salt. Set aside. Cream shortening and butter. Add sugars and mix until light and fluffy. Add vanilla and eggs, blending well. Shape dough into balls and roll in sugar. Place on baking sheet.

Bake at 350 for 12 minutes. Immediately top each cookie with 3 candy coated chocolate Easter eggs, pressing firmly.

Cookies & Considerations:

If you have troubles getting the eggs to stick, try baking the cookies without rolling them in sugar. Or tell the kids to be careful - they are eggs, after all.

"Hope is the thing with feathers that perches in the soul."
Emily Dickinson

Getting Kicked in the Proverbial Teeth

The only difficulty with wanting to see the best in people, especially people we think of as friends, is that sometimes, someone comes along who really challenges your way of thinking.

We try to believe that people are honorable, sincere and trustworthy. Part of the half full, half empty philosophy, we prefer to think that people are basically good. But sometimes people say and do things that hurt us and cause us to doubt our own wisdom and question our beliefs.

When we give people the benefit of the doubt, it's possible that they'll take our trust, and employ malicious, vengeful and deceitful behavior in return. So it is that many times, when we're kicked in the proverbial teeth, abused, taken advantage of, betrayed and violated, we ask ourselves "How could they do that?"

We can't answer that question. We don't know enough about the lessons others have yet to learn and it's not for us to judge.

When things go wrong, it's human nature to apply the easier principle of judgment. But easier isn't always better, it's just easier. It may be much more difficult to focus on forgiveness and understanding, but our most valuable opportunities to learn often come from our toughest lessons.

Few of us arrive knowing all we need to know. We all have lessons to learn and weaknesses to overcome. We know our own strengths and weaknesses better than anyone does.

We also know what we're made of, our ideals and our intent. We know our beliefs and our character, what's in our hearts and in our conscience.

Focusing on ourselves helps us understand that when others hurt us, when friends let us down, when we are betrayed, it's just another lesson we need to learn, so that we can let go and move on to other lessons and challenges.

One of our greatest challenges is to cease worrying about things that are beyond the power of our wishes. What others do, is beyond our power. What we do, is not.

We shouldn't let past hurts blind us to virtue. Life is too short to hold grudges. Releasing judgment and concentrating on forgiveness and understanding will set us free.

When someone hurts us, we can continue to challenge our way of thinking by offering acceptance, forgiveness, guidance, hope, understanding and love. It might or might not help them, but it almost certainly will help us.

Food for thought:
". . . Exercise caution . . . for the world is full of trickery. But let this not blind you to what virtue there is; many persons strive for high ideals; and every-where life is full of heroism.
Be yourself. Especially do not feign affection. Neither be cynical about love; for in the face of all aridity and disenchantment
it is perennial as the grass. . .
Be gentle with yourself. . .
And whether or not it is clear to you, no doubt the universe is unfolding as it should. . .
Keep peace with your soul.
With all it's sham, drudgery and broken dreams, it is still a beautiful world.
Be cheerful. Strive to be happy."
Excerpts from Desiderata©
Written in 1927 by Max Ehrmann

Challenge!

Pecan Butterballs
Cookies & Considerations
on following page.

Pecan Butterballs

2 cups flour
1 tsp. salt
3 cups finely ground pecans
1 cup butter
3/4 cup sugar
2 tsp. vanilla
approx. 3 cups icing sugar for rolling

Combine flour, salt and pecans. Set aside. Cream butter and sugar. Add vanilla. Blend in flour/nut mixture. Form into 1" balls or crescents.

Bake at 300 for 25 - 30 minutes or till firm. While still hot, roll cookies in icing sugar. Cool and sprinkle with more icing sugar.

Cookies & Considerations:

Last week, someone I thought of as a friend let me down. He probably doesn't know how much he hurt me, but I'll give him the benefit of the doubt and forgive him anyway.

Sometimes called snowballs, nuggets, Greek Butterballs or Mexican Wedding Cookies, sometimes with rum, tequila, or other nuts - these little round cookies won't let you down. Whether you shape them into balls or crescents, they'll hold their shape. Challenge your way of thinking by flavoring the icing sugar with a vanilla bean, before rolling these cookies in it.

Banana Cream Pie Sandwich Cookies

Cookie:
2 & 1/3 cups flour
1 cup sugar
1 cup butter
1/2 cup banana, cut into 1/4 inch slices
1/4 tsp. salt
1 tsp. vanilla
1/2 cup chopped pecans

Filling:
3 cups icing sugar
1/3 cup butter
4 Tbsp. whipping cream
1 tsp. vanilla

Cookie:
      Combine all ingredients in a large mixer bowl and beat on low until well mixed (2 - 3 minutes). Shape into 1 inch balls and place on greased cookie sheets. Flatten each cookie to 1/4 inch thickness, with the bottom of a glass that has been dipped in sugar.
      Bake at 350 for 12 - 15 minutes or until edges are light brown. Cool completely.

Filling:
      Combine all ingredients in mixer bowl and beat until light and fluffy. Spread 1 Tbsp. of filling over the bottom of half the cookies. Top with remaining cookies.

Cookies & Considerations:
      The taste of bananas if very subtle. This makes a surprisingly crispy, crunchy, nutty cookie -quite unique.

Honey -
The Computer Shrunk My Connection to Real People!

Well toss me in a bowl and call me salad, 'cause when it comes to communicating on the Internet, I'm about as green as it gets!

Until recently, I thought "cookies" were those things you took "bytes" of and "Yahoo!" was something you hollered during the Calgary Stampede! Now, I'm starting to see that I'll be eating greens for a while. It's a good thing I like salad.

The Internet is an immense general reference network of information and communication, providing access, world wide, to over half a million websites.

For someone as green as me, it can be a little overwhelming trying to decide where to go. It's like trying to figure out what to watch on t. v. when there are thousands of channels to choose from, and no point of reference. How do you find something of interest? It's tempting to just plop down in front of the screen saver, let the eyes glaze over, and nibble on a bit of rubber lettuce. Welcome to cyber-space!

It would seem that, with all these advanced technological communication devices, we'd all be pretty well connected. Besides the Internet and email, we have faxes and modems, cell phones, cordless phones, phones in our cars, phones in our homes, videophones, beepers, voice mail and good, old-fashioned postal mail.

But when our connections to others are typed on a keyboard or spoken over the phone, we may be forfeiting part of the communiqué.

If we normally motion with our hands and arms, how can we send those gestures over the phone? How do we send body language and make eye contact through the mail? Can a personal scent or a casual caress be relayed by the click of a button? Do we double click to transmit a tilt of the head and left click to send inflections and accents in our speech? Can we voice mail a tear or a twinkle in our eyes or fax a smile, a chuckle or a frown? How do we send hugs and enthusiasm without using letters and symbols that the spell checker will pick up? Would the grammar checker suitably communicate the opportunity to unexpectedly make a new connection at a seemingly chance encounter?

We want, and need, to be connected to others. A meaningful way of communicating and connecting goes beyond passing on words - it involves all of our senses . . . and more.

Genuine communication involves energy, actions and good intentions. If our intentions are centered on positive energy, thoughtful understanding and conscious actions, we will convey, from our hearts and souls, what we want to say.

Like a well organized web page, we are exquisitely linked to each other. Uniquely intertwined in a real time slow dance, we sway to the choreographed music of our soul's needs. Allowing our souls to blend with others all around the world provides us with the opportunity to show love.

And love is the real World Wide Web that links us all.

Food for thought:
"The world community can exist only with world communication, which means something more than extensive shortwave facilities scattered about the globe. It means common understanding, a common tradition, common ideas, and common ideals."
Robert M. Hutchins

Connect!

ABC (Absolute Best Chewy) Chocolate Chippers
Cookies & Considerations
on following page.

ABC (Absolute Best Chewy) Chocolate Chippers

3 cups flour
1 tsp. salt
1 tsp. baking soda
1/4 tsp. baking powder
3/4 cup butter
1 cup brown sugar
1/2 cup sugar
1 Tbsp. vanilla
2 eggs
2 Tbsp. corn syrup
1 Tbsp. cream
2 cups chocolate chips
   or chunks
1 cup chopped nuts

Combine flour, salt, baking soda and baking powder. Cream butter and sugars. Add vanilla. Add eggs, one at a time, beating well. Beat in corn syrup and cream. Add flour mixture. Stir in chocolate chips and nuts. Drop onto cookie sheets and flatten slightly.

Bake at 350 for 10 - 12 minutes or until golden brown around edges.

Cookies & Considerations:

Typing in "cookies", at just two of the search engines for the Internet was a bit overwhelming - 251 sites popped up during one search and "Yahoo!" found over 600 sites featuring cookies (some real, some virtual).

After checking the first 20, my eyes started to glaze over. As I reached for my salad, I found a cute way to email a "digital" cookie to someone, when you can't make the connection in person.

But they had no recipes, so I went to another site, where I found this recipe for a traditional, common, world-wide popular, chewy chocolate chip cookies. This is the modified version.

Bear's Paws

1 - 397 gram pkg. puff pastry (or homemade)
1/2 cup butter
1/2 cup sugar
1/2 cup ground almonds
1/2 tsp. almond extract
1 cup icing sugar
1 tsp. vanilla
1/2 cup whipping cream

Thaw puff pastry if frozen. Cream together butter and sugar. Add almonds and flavoring. Mix well. Set aside. For the glaze, combine icing sugar, vanilla, and enough cream to make a drizzling consistency. Set aside. Roll our puff pastry to 12" x 12". Cut in 4" x 2" rectangles. Place 1 tsp. of filling in center of each and fold lengthwise, sealing edges with water. Snip on long edge 3 times.

Bake on parchment paper (they'll leak!), at 400 for 8 minutes. Immediately brush with glaze and devour.

Cookies & Considerations:

Every home needs the unconditional love of a cuddly bear. Dickens is the most loved and special bear in our home. He's no ordinary bear, and these are no ordinary cookies. More like a pastry, they're small, like a little cookie and a little bear named Dickens.

Harvest Month

The changes in nature are once more yielding to a new season. For many, September is traditionally thought of as harvest month - the time of gathering together.

The essence of the season is distinguished by a conspicuous flurry of harvesting in our orchards, fields and gardens. Our own small, hastily planted plot, will yield 2 beans, 19 cherry tomatoes (all smaller than a marble - 5 smaller than a pea) and a half a square foot of 1" high lettuce (I'm not sure what kind, and I don't think it really matters). It's not exactly a bumper crop, but at least it won't nearly kill the horses to bring it all in!

Thankfully, due to the richness and availability of fresh produce year round, our need to be self-sufficient, to preserve, freeze, dry and otherwise squirrel away fruits and vegetables, has changed. Our need to grow things has not.

Many of us still dream of a garden, often purely for pleasure. Refreshment for our souls, we desire our gardens to encircle our homes, guarding our palaces and castles like lush, green moats.

Scented flowers, aromatic herbs, a fruit tree or two, a vegetable garden, a salad garden, a wild garden, a flower garden, bright berry bushes, a greenhouse, hedges - a garden is a very personal thing. No two are alike. What we grow in our garden is determined by the space it will occupy, the time and money we have to invest, the soil, what we like to eat and, of course, the length and temperature of our growing season.

In September, the profound effects of seasonal changes are nature's signal to harvest, sow and scatter. In anticipation of fall, plants shed their leaves, seeds put on hardy winter coats to keep out the cold and buds wrap themselves in wax to protect themselves against ice and snow.

Virtually every living thing is affected by the seasons.

The close of another season of growing, sowing, and harvesting, arrives with the urgent necessity for us to give thanks. With such a plenitude of fresh vegetables and an abundance of fruits at the farmer's markets, country fairs, and even in our own back yards, it's easy to take for granted how grateful we need to be for all that we have to eat. In other parts of the world there is famine, drought, starvation and rations. We are fortunate that we live in a part of the world where there is plenty, when elsewhere, there are many in need.

This month, next month and all year round, there are many blessings to be harvested. And what a harvest it could be if we were all grateful for what has been provided.

Food for thought:
"Let those love now who never loved before,
Whilst those who always loved, love even more.
Let all who feel rejected, seek and find
New hope, new warmth and healing peace of mind.
Let those who think their faith has ebbed away
Stretch out their hands, to grasp a brighter day.
Let those who are imprisoned, far and wide,
Find freedom, where all men walk side by side.
Let those who have abundant blessings, give
To those in dark despair, the will to live.
Let all who love, now sow and reap and share
The harvest of the Spirit - everywhere."
Iris Hesselden

Harvest!

Harvest
Cookies & Considerations
on following page.

Harvest Cookies

2 & 1/2 cups whole wheat flour
2 cups old-fashioned, large flake, rolled oats
1/2 cup dry milk powder
1/2 cup wheat germ
2 tsp. baking powder
1 tsp. baking soda
2 tsp. cinnamon
1 tsp. ginger
1/2 tsp. salt
1/2 cup oil
3 eggs
1/2 cup molasses
1/4 cup honey
2 apples, diced
1/2 cup raisins

Combine whole wheat flour, oats, dry milk powder, wheat germ, baking powder, baking soda, cinnamon, ginger and salt. Set aside. In a large bowl, whisk together oil, eggs, molasses and honey. Stir in flour mixture. Add apples and raisins. Drop on greased baking sheet and flatten slightly.

Bake at 350 for 10 - 12 minutes.

Cookies & Considerations:

I give thanks for the bounties that are supplied for my enjoyment. Each day, and especially on this day, I'm grateful for the ingredients that go into these low-fat, low sugar, low cholesterol, high fiber, nutritious, soft, eat em any time of the day or year, Harvest Cookies.

Apricot Crescents

Filling:
2 cups dried apricots
2 cups sugar
1/2 tsp. cinnamon

Cookies:
3 cups whole wheat flour
2 & 1/2 cups oatmeal
1/2 tsp. baking soda
1 cup butter
1 cup brown sugar
1/2 cup sugar
1 tsp. maple or vanilla flavoring
2 eggs
1/4 cup milk

Filling:
Cook apricots in water until soft. Drain well. Stir in sugar and cinnamon. Cook until mixture becomes smooth. Cool completely.

Cookies:
Combine flour, oatmeal and baking soda. Set aside. Cream together butter, sugars and flavoring. Add eggs and milk. Stir in flour mixture. Roll out dough to 1/4" thickness. Cut in 2" rounds and place on greased or parchment lined cookie sheet. Place 1 tsp. of filling on each round and cover with other half of the round sealing edges and pushing the filling down to make a level sandwich. Add more milk if necessary.
Bake at 350 for 12 - 15 minutes or until lightly browned.

Cookies & Considerations:
The filling is tasty, but it burns easily so keep an eye on it when cooking with the sugar added. (Or substitute with regular jam.)

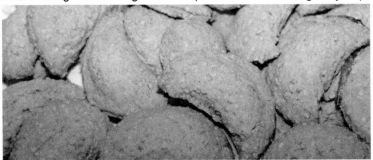

How Much Are You Worth?

"If you're searching desperately for the meaning of life, try the floor of my car, because there's a lot of crap down there!" But if you're searching for the meaning of self-worth, this may help.

How do you measure your self-worth?

Is it how much you have? Is it your net income?

When you fill out the part of the questionnaire that asks your annual income what do you check or circle? 0 - $10,000, 10-50K, 50-100K . . . more? Or less? Do you view your life as a cheap commodity?

In the material world, it's easy to associate our self-worth with the amount of money we have in the bank, the limit on our credit cards, our net assets and the sum of our personal possessions.

Still, what if the world's currency was suddenly based only on self-worth?

What if all value placed on physical belongings, ceased to exist, and you were judged only on self-value. Do you think you'd have the collateral you'd need to borrow for a lifetime?

Could you market yourself on the recollection of the reverence you had for life, including your ability to honor, appreciate and show love, to all of those in it? Would you be able to barter a loan, based on the exchange of accumulated prayers from family and friends?

Could your sense of humor and personality be an endorsement for a long line of credit? Could you negotiate a small loan based on your ability to show feeling, maintain a positive attitude and cope with stress?

How would you calculate a fair market value for your health, well being and happiness?

While at the bank, could you withdraw funds from the stash of kindness, caring and compassion you've shown strangers? Could you secure financing for your next major purchase by peddling tolerance, understanding and patience? Is your awareness, empathy and consideration of others a creditable exchange for next week's groceries?

Would your appreciation for beauty and the power of nature, and your gentleness with the earth and other living creatures, sound like a bargain to someone who might advance you some legal tender?

Could an estimate of value and worth be imparted, based on your firmly established awareness of the richness, fullness and abundance that flows through you, from a higher power?

Could you victoriously acquire a mortgage based on your knowledge that each encounter with another soul, is a higher power's way of saying thank you for your help?

Would an independent appraiser be able to assess your capacity to fulfill a fiscal promise, based on your blessings and good wishes for others - even those you don't understand?

Maybe not.

But maybe when we are able to do all those things, while bestowing a silent blessing (or two) on the people and circumstances that come into our lives, without expecting a penny in return, we will have learnt that all of those are redeemable assets.

We don't have to sell ourselves in order to know and honor our self-worth. Our true worth is not based on fiscal commodities, encumbrances and accouterments, at all. We are all valuable because of whom we are, not because of how much we have or because of the car we drive. We are all special and priceless, not because of the homes we live in or the things in our homes. We should all be honored and revered, not because of the clothes we wear or the labels on them, but for the powerful spirits that we are.

Ultimately, that will mean more than all of our corporeal possessions combined.

Food for thought:
"You can't sell yourself, because you're priceless."
Terry Lynn Taylor & Mary Beth Crain

Revere!

Maple Spice
Cookies & Considerations
on following page.

Maple Spice Cookies

5 cups flour
1 tsp. baking soda
2 tsp. cinnamon
1/2 tsp. ground cloves
1/2 tsp. ground allspice
1/2 tsp. ground nutmeg
1/2 tsp. ground ginger
1/2 tsp. salt
1 cup butter
1 cup brown sugar
2 eggs
1 cup maple syrup (imitation works!)
2 Tbsp. molasses
1 tsp. grated orange zest
cinnamon sugar (or sugar) for rolling

Combine flour, baking soda, cinnamon, cloves, allspice, nutmeg, ginger and salt. Set aside. Cream butter and sugar. Beat in eggs and add maple syrup, molasses, and orange zest. Gradually add the flour mixture.

Drop by spoonfuls into sugar and roll. Place on lightly greased baking sheets and flatten.

Bake at 350 for 12 minutes, or until the color of an old copper penny.

Cookies & Considerations:

If the world were to suddenly need a new currency, these soft cookies, with an aromatic blend of maple syrup, molasses, orange zest and spices, would make a wonderful, priceless, legal tender - the color of a well seasoned copper penny.

Peanut Butter & Cream Yo-Yo Cookies

Cookie:
1 & 1/2 cups flour
1 tsp. baking soda
1 tsp. salt
1/2 tsp. baking powder
2 cup rolled oats
1 cup butter
1 cup peanut butter
1 cup sugar
1 cup brown sugar
2 eggs
1 tsp. vanilla
2 eggs

Filling:
2 cups icing sugar
6 T. butter
1 cup peanut butter
1/4 cup whipping cream

Combine flour, baking soda, salt, baking powder and rolled oats. Set aside. Cream butter and peanut butter. Add both sugars and mix well. Add eggs and vanilla. Blend in flour & oats mixture. Shape dough into small balls and place on parchment lined cookie sheets.

Bake at 350 for 10 - 12 minutes or until golden. Cool completely while preparing the filling:

Filling:

Combine all ingredients until fluffy. Turn half the cookies upside down and spread with 1 tsp. of filling. Top with another cookie. Devour or refrigerate.

Cookies & Considerations:

A great tasting and easy to make sandwich cookie that's sure to be a hit with the peanut butter crowd.

Readjusting - A Round of Mini Golf

We've all heard (and possibly even used) the excuse "my dog ate my homework". Well, it's happened to me (with some minor modifications).

What ignorant bliss, to be oblivious to the perils of the day ahead - especially those that could easily have been avoided. There were certainly measures I could have taken and choices I could have made. And I knew it! Admittedly, I was a co-conspirator.

My computer didn't just eat my column - I set the table, laid out the food and rang the dinner bell!

Following that, I engaged in a few choice words, slammed some doors, banged some dishes, and generally stomped about in an utterly ridiculous and completely haphazard sequence. My outburst had succeeded, in its unique and sole purpose. I still didn't have my column but my blood pressure could tell a tale or two! As I staggered to a halt, I readjusted, retraced, reflected and repeated (many times) my zestful new mantra.

"We already have everything that we need."

Dwelling on that heartening bit of wisdom, I got out my disc, restarted my column from scratch, and saved as I went!

Like a round of mini golf, our lives are sometimes an untidy jumble of obstacles to go over, around and through - some small, some big, some easy, some mission impossible!

The game, we know, is a lot of fun, but there are going to be obstacles. We never know when troubles on the course will require us to use our expertise and inventiveness to accommodate, reorganize and integrate a new strategy, including, possibly, the selection of a new path or plan.

Sometimes we're able to pick up the golf ball and start where we left off. Sometimes we need to start all over. Sometimes we can wait it out, letting someone else play through, and sometimes we are forced to turn around and try another route.

It is a common dilemma to be taken aback, as we flounder to reconcile ourselves to the unexpected events of the day. How often we are challenged to proceed with what we've started, readjusting as we go. Seldom are we prepared or equipped for the next inconvenience that life submits for our approval.

When the obstacles we encounter are vastly different from what we would have preferred, it's time to readjust. Repeat after me:

"We already have everything that we need."

We carry within us the strength, wisdom and courage to handle whatever life demands of us.

We often begin without a clear view of what we want to achieve, where to go, and what we'll find when we get there. Sometimes the only thing we know is that there is greater risk in not doing anything at all.

Even without knowing in which direction to move, we are able to advance on the strength of faith. Artistry, aptitude and skill come from unlikely sources and at opportune moments, casting our doubts aside and making readjustments possible.

Reach up. All things are possible with love, trust and faith. We already have everything that we need. All we need to do is ask.

Food for thought:
"Within us all there are wells of thought and dynamos of energy which are not suspected until emergencies arise. Then oftentimes we find that it is comparatively simple to double or triple our former capacities and to amaze ourselves by the results achieved."
Thomas J. Watson

Readjust!

Sugarless Chocolate Chip Oatmeal
Cookies & Considerations
on following page.

Sugarless Chocolate Chip Oatmeal Cookies

1 cup whole wheat flour
1 & 1/4 cups white flour
2 cups powdered artificial sweetener (or 1 Tbsp. Stevia®*)
1/2 tsp. salt
2 tsp. baking soda
4 cups rolled oats
1 cup oil
2 cups hot water
1 tsp. vanilla
1/2 cup finely chopped walnuts
1 cup sugar free carob chips*

*Most carob chips are lightly sweetened with whole grain malted barley and corn. They may contain palm kernel oil.

Combine flours, sweetener, salt, baking soda and rolled oats. In a large bowl, blend oil, water, and vanilla. Add flour mixture. Blend in walnuts and carob chips. Drop onto lightly greased cookie sheets. Flatten.
Bake at 325 for 15 minutes. (Color will not change noticeably.)

Cookies & Considerations:
Something Diabetics and other people with sugar intolerance have to do quite often in readjust the foods they eat, particularly the amount of sugar they use.
*These cookies can also be made with Stevia®, a little known herbal sugar replacement, only recently garnering increased attention in North America. Research is still being done, but at up to 400 times sweeter than sugar, Stevia is a viable, natural substitute for people wishing to readjust the amount of sugar they consume. Look for it at your local health food store.

Ginger Chews (Low Fat)

3 cups flour
1 tsp. baking soda
1 tsp. ground ginger
1 tsp. cinnamon
1 tsp. cloves
1 tsp. allspice
1 tsp. nutmeg
1/4 tsp. salt
1/2 cup brown sugar (or sugar substitute, but they'll be dryer!)
2 Tbsp. margarine or butter
3/4 cup molasses
1/3 cup apple juice

Combine flour, baking soda, spices and salt. Set aside. Beat the brown sugar, margarine or butter and molasses, till smooth. Add the apple juice and beat again. Add the flour mixture and beat till well mixed. Drop onto baking sheets sprayed with nonstick cooking spray. Flatten slightly.

Bake at 350 for 10 - 12 minutes or till done.

Cookies & Considerations:

These low fat cookies are so moist and tasty, you won't even notice they're low in fat.

Juicy Fruits and Sweet Surprises

What do these fruits have in common with the people in your life?

Pineapples: They're prickly and tough (like a pine cone). They have thick, green and golden, pointy skin and a stiff, spiky crown. Inside, they're juicy, sweet and ready to eat.

Lychee nuts: They're smallish, reddish brown, hard round balls. They have a thin, crunchy, warty, bark-like skin, and stiff, woody branches. Inside, they're juicy, sweet and ready to eat.

Mangoes: They're kind of an oval or kidney shape. They have smooth red, orange or yellow, leathery skin. Inside, they're juicy, sweet and ready to eat.

Kiwis: They're shaped like an egg, but softer. They have thin, furry brown skin. Inside, they're juicy, sweet and ready to eat.

Casaba melons: They're big, firm, and heavy, with an acorn top on the blossom end. They have thick yellow and green skin with deep ridges. Inside, they're juicy, sweet, and ready to eat.

Figs: They're green and brownish black. They are shaped like a teardrop. Inside, they're juicy sweet, and ready to eat.

Like all of these fruits, we can think of the people in our lives, in terms of how well we've gotten to know them.

With zest, we feast mainly on morsels that smack of tangy familiarity. Our friendships are customarily based on our visual preference, much like the fruit we eat.

Often times people appear to be a little standoffish. Like the pineapple, they may seem stiff and prickly. Possibly, they seem grouchy and a tad unfriendly. It could be that, on the surface, people resemble the lychee and melon - hard and unyielding. Perhaps they act defensive or overly guarded. Maybe they're too smooth and unusual, like the mango and the kiwi.

Like the fruits, we frequently tend to judge people by their outer appearances. Shyness, a natural, reserved nature, or circumstances in their present day, also make people the way they are. Instead of taking it personally we should hold our interpretations. Like the fruit, we choose to make judgments, jump to conclusions and create assumptions based on outer appearances. When we're tempted to make a judgment, we should remember that we are not here to judge. Instead, we would do well to concentrate on savoring, with as much relish as we can muster, tiny tidbits and dainty samples of all the flavors of humanity.

Instead of seeing other individuals as difficult to approach, with patience, we might find that, hidden underneath the prickly and curious looking exterior, we discover a person waiting to surprise and delight us. Whether or not we're willing to get to know them better is often dependent on how willing we are to pierce their exterior. Only then will we be permitted to discover what's really inside.

All food is good for you. Be adventuresome and willing to explore new things. Eat what makes you happy, but challenge your way of thinking every now and then. Keep an open mind, and don't be afraid when the people in your life look a little different on the outside.

Food for thought:
"The best and most beautiful things in the world cannot be seen, nor touched, but felt in the heart."
Helen Keller

Explore!

Chocolate Shortbread Fruit Pizza
Cookies & Considerations
on following page.

Chocolate Shortbread Fruit Pizza

1 & 1/2 cups flour
1/2 cup cocoa
1/2 tsp. salt
1 cup butter
1/2 cup brown sugar
1/3 cup icing sugar

Combine flour, cocoa and salt. Set aside. Cream butter. Add sugars and mix. Add flour mixture and beat until dough forms a ball. Press onto bottom of a pizza pan. Bake at 350 for 15 - 18 minutes or till done. Cool Completely.

Topping:
1 - 250 gram pkg. cream cheese or light cream cheese
1/2 cup sugar
1 tsp. vanilla
assorted fresh fruit

Glaze:
Melt 1/4 cup of apricot jam or orange marmalade with 1 Tbsp. water.

Beat cheese. Add sugar and vanilla. Mix until fluffy. Spread over cooled crust and arrange a variety of fresh fruit on top. Glaze if desired. Drizzle with chocolate if desired. Garnish with whipped cream if desired. Cut into wedges.

Cookies & Considerations:
Summer is such an incredibly abundant time. There is such a richness of flavors and textures waiting to tempt your taste buds and tease your palette. Experiment with some new fresh fruits this summer. Use some as a topping on this big cookie you cut up.

Macadamia & Coconut Crescents

2 & 1/4 cups flour
1 tsp. salt
1 cup butter
3/4 cup icing sugar
1 tsp. vanilla
1 cup chopped, roasted & salted macadamia nuts
1/2 cup toasted coconut
extra icing sugar

Combine flour and salt and set aside. Beat butter until light. Gradually add icing sugar and vanilla. Add flour mixture. Add nuts and coconut. Shape dough into 2" long, 1/2" round logs and curve into crescents.

Bake at 325 for 15 - 20 minutes or till golden. Immediately dust with icing sugar. Cool and dust with icing sugar again.

Cookies & Considerations:

Who can resist a crunchy macadamia nut? These are hard to resist too, with a hint of coconut - a crispy, tasty blend.

Jo-Jo - The Bird With Attitude

We found Jo-Jo lying on the slushy sidewalk downtown.

While other pedestrians stepped around the plastic bag identifying the store where he was originally purchased, I found myself impulsively eager to inspect the contents of that translucent bag. Whatever it was, it was green and orange, and I was intuitively drawn to it.

Walking over, we gently nudged the bag with the toe of a booted foot.

"I think it's balloons," my son said, drinking noisily from his Slurpie.

"It can't be," I replied, "it has fur."

I juggled the yield of our excursion to town - a newspaper, two magazines, another Slurpie and a couple of shopping bags, including some salt & vinegar potato chips, a 4 liter jug of milk and a grass angel. We picked up the bag on the sidewalk and guarding our newfound treasure possessively, hastily peeked inside.

That's how we met "Jo-Jo - The Bird With Attitude"!

Jo-Jo has florescent green fake-fur and neon orange feet and bill. He is a puppet whose tag says he squeaks when you open his mouth. It's true that it does, although at the moment, he's sitting quietly in front of me with his big round tag flopped over his left eye, his green fur (feathers?!) flopped over his right eye, feet dangling and beak liberally protruding.

Even though Jo-Jo has been labeled "the meanest, biggest mouthed, puppet bird you've ever seen", for the time being, he doesn't appear to have much of an attitude at all. Actually, we like Jo-Jo so much that if his owner doesn't claim him, we'll clip his tag and let him spread his hairy green wings and fly, squeaking the whole time.

Whatever else Jo-Jo may or may not be, he is an inspiration.

"Jo-Jo, The Bird With Attitude", along with the rest of us, have many choices in life. Attitude is one of life's choices.

Attitude, it is said, is everything. Change your attitude and you change the world - or at least, the world as you see it.

For most of us, it's rare to be 100% immune to outside influences. Often, when coping with unavoidable stresses, we're likely to experience a number of emotions including intimidation, worry, uncertainty, discouragement, disappointment, rejection, invalidation, insecurity, disparagement and the feeling that we are unloved and unappreciated. It's somewhat inevitable that, from time to time, our self-esteem, confidence and positive attitudes are discounted, and offered at bargain basement prices.

Although we don't generally have control over the events in our lives, we do have control over our responses to them.

A situation we can't change is the same situation whether we have a positive attitude or not. The art of pessimism, like any other personality trait, can be modified, if that is what we choose to do. Just as pessimism is learnt, we can also learn to be optimistic. Choosing a positive attitude may not solve our problems, but it might rid us of some negative perceptions that bring hopelessness and despair.

Optimism, along with an open and accepting attitude, helps us deal with changes, unavoidable problems, difficulties and adversities - both emotional and physical. Many doctors now believe that a positive attitude can be the single most important factor in profoundly bolstering our health, helping us heal, and prolonging our lives.

A confident attitude, that is full of self esteem, might not be easy everyday, but developing an attitude that is resistant to collapse is a good way to alter our lives.

In life, we choose our own reality. Attitude is one of life's choices.

Food for thought:
"The greatest discovery of any generation is that human beings can alter their lives by altering the attitudes of their minds."
Albert Schweitzer

Choose!

Jo-Jo Birders
Cookies & Considerations
on following page.

Jo-Jo Birders

4 & 1/2 cups flour
1 tsp. baking powder
1 tsp. baking soda
1 tsp. salt
2 tsp. ginger
2 tsp. cinnamon
1/2 tsp. cloves
1/2 tsp. allspice
1/2 tsp. nutmeg
3/4 cup butter
1 cup brown sugar
1 cup molasses
1/2 cup water

Combine flour, baking powder, baking soda, salt and spices. Set aside. Cream butter and brown sugar. Add molasses and water. Gradually blend in flour mixture. Chill 1 hour. On a floured surface, roll dough to 1/4" thickness, and cut with 3" cookie cutters.

Bake at 350 for 10 - 12 minutes or till firm.

Cookies & Considerations:

Perk up someone else's attitude by sharing your excitement for life. Choose to show kindness to others. Bolster someone's self-esteem by telling them they're special and that you care. Instill confidence in someone by telling them that you love them - unconditionally!

A family member recently said to me, "You want to see things all happy, and I want to see the bad stuff." I agree with that assessment. My attitude is my choice! Squeak, if you agree!!

Usually called Jo Froggers, these cookies puff up like birds as they bake. After, they flatten out to a cutout cookie that's full of flavor and marvelous attitude.

Brazil Nut Biscotti

2 cups flour
3/4 cup sugar
1/2 tsp. cinnamon
2 tsp. baking powder
1/2 tsp. salt
3 eggs
2 tsp. vanilla
2 cups whole brazil nuts

Combine flour, sugar, cinnamon, baking powder and salt in a large bowl. Add eggs and vanilla. Stir in brazil nuts. Knead dough on a lightly floured surface for 1 - 2 minutes. Divide dough in half and shape each half into a 12" log. Place on parchment lined baking sheet and press down gently to flatten logs to 1" high, by 2" wide.

Bake at 350 for 30 minutes. Cool. Slice logs diagonally into 1/4" thick slices. Place on cookie sheet, standing up if possible and bake 10 - 15 minutes, or till golden and crisp.

Cookies & Considerations:
A tasty, crunchy version, with big chunks of brazil nuts.

People who have never made biscotti have a phobia about them. They are very easy to make and very forgiving, but you do have to enjoy the crunch, or dunking, to enjoy a true biscotti.

i souport publik edekashun.

"i souport publik edekashun."

Aside from being another way to misspell "public", it's one of a whole swack of bumper stickers my sister sent me, retrieved off the Internet.

I also like "Time is what keeps everything from happening at once." and "Okay, who stopped payment on my reality check?"

But my favorites are "Warning: Dates in calendar are closer than they appear." and "Out of my mind. Back in five minutes."

As well, I got these "Dilbert's Words of Wisdom", from a friend: "I love deadlines. I especially like the whooshing sound they make as they go flying by." and "I don't suffer from stress. I'm a carrier."

It's a humorous way to poke fun at ourselves. In doing so, we acknowledge the stresses that multi-tasking and lack of time have created.

New inventions coming out to help facilitate that are televisions that offer viewing on 12 screens simultaneously and devises that allow us to cruise the net and the highway at the same time. We eat at the computer while talking on the phone between mouthfuls. Even a de-stresser, like working out at the gym, can become multi-tasked when we try to read, watch t. v. or check our email while we use the treadmill, stair climber or exercycle.

We're over-stimulated, stressed and preoccupied.

Technological advances have meant that we experience and encounter more. But instead of slowing down and becoming more efficient, we've become more disorderly at a higher rate of speed.

We all have our own stresses, and our own ways of dealing with stress. Humor is a great way to relieve stress, but when the rent is due, we've lost your work sheet with the list of things we're supposed to do, we're being audited, we misspell one little word in the local paper and we just can't laugh, it's time to turn to . . . faith and chocolate!

And why not? In keeping with the theme of multi-tasking, we can practice faith while eating chocolate because in 1753, botanist Carolus Linnaeus gave the cacao tree the botanical name Theobroma. It means "food of the gods."

As far as edibles go, chocolate is widely popular. For centuries, chocolate was used mainly as a beverage. Nowadays, people everywhere also enjoy chocolate in the form of candies and pastries. In fact, ask someone what their favorite kind of cookie is and 95% will say the word "chocolate", shortly followed by the word "chip". (Figures are not based on a current poll conducted by anyone, as far as I know. They're just a wild guess and the results of my own minuscule, unscientific study!)

Take a moment to consider these benefits though:

Doctors now report that people who eat chocolate three times a month (that's month - not day) may be adding an entire year to their lives! Antioxidants, they say, are worthy of the credit. At 410mg, a three ounce portion of high-quality Swiss chocolate, gets you more disease fighting antitoxins than a serving of broccoli! (Sorry, broccoli.)

Presently, U. S. confectioners are marketing a chocolate bar to health conscious and environmentally aware Americans. Peaceworks introduced the chocolate bars, which promote peace in the Middle East, a short while ago, in Chicago. "WAFA" chocolate bars are made by unified Arabs and Israelis, hoping to assist efforts for world peace through the sale of their chocolate bars. One tenth of the proceeds go towards teaching young people, associated with the organization Seeds of Peace, about coexistence.

The Endangered Species Chocolate Company donates a quarter of all profits to environmental causes, one of which plans to plant 20 million trees by year 2000. The company, located in Talent, Oregon, sells organic chocolate called "Bug Bites". The chocolates come with collectible insect trading cards that teach how to replace chemical fertilizers and pesticides, with organic farming and insects.

So go ahead, I say. Let's eat chocolate!

Not only will we be getting a healthy dose of antioxidants, but we can promote world peace, help plant trees, learn about organic farming and insects, beat stress and please the God's!

And that's right in keeping with the fundamental principle of multi-tasking!

Food for Thought:
"Research tells us that fourteen out of any ten people like chocolate."
Sandra Boynton

Coexist!

Black & Whites
Cookies & Considerations
on following page.

Black & Whites

4 & 1/2 cups flour
1 & 1/2 cups cocoa
2 tsp. baking soda
1 tsp. salt
2 & 1/2 cups butter
4 cups sugar
4 eggs
2 tsp. vanilla
3 cups (600 grams) white chocolate, coarsely chopped (or chips)

Combine flour, cocoa, baking soda, and salt. Set aside. Cream butter and sugar. Add eggs and vanilla. Gradually add flour mixture. Beat well. Add white chocolate chunks. Drop onto baking sheet
Bake at 350 for 10 minutes.

Cookies & Considerations:

Besides being dark, fudgey and chewy, with big chunks of white chocolate, these double-chocolate cookies are full of antioxidants. They're also a good example of opposing factions coexisting in peace. Now, if only we could get a whole swack of them over to the Balkans, we might really see world peace!

"Real religion is a way of life, not a white cloak to be wrapped around us on the Sabbath and then cast aside into the six-day closet of unconcern."
William Arthur Ward

Real (Snappy) Gingersnaps

2 cups flour
1 tsp. baking soda
1/2 tsp. salt
2 tsp. ginger
1 tsp. cinnamon
1 tsp. allspice
1 tsp. cloves
1 cup sugar
1/2 cup oil
1 egg
1/2 cup molasses

Combine flour, soda, salt and spices. Set aside. Mix the sugar, oil, egg and molasses well. Add flour mixture. Roll into small balls and place on greased cookie sheet.

Bake at 350 for 12 - 15 minutes or till done.

Cookies & Considerations:

The real thing! Real snappy for dunking! Better make a double batch!

If I could give only one piece of advice about cookies in this entire book, that works for most cookies, it would be don't over-bake them. Having said that, disregard it, because it doesn't apply for this cookie. If you want it to be crispy, dunkable and snappy, over-bake it a bit. If you want chewy, take them out sooner.

I Said a Prayer for You Today

Last week, I had a date with approximately 200 students, 10 parents and 4 teachers. At the Children's Festival in Calgary, our throng blended with many others.

While we were there, we saw two plays.

One was called Swan's Down. It was put on by a theater company from the Netherlands and was about a family and a pair of swans who all lived on a canal.

The other play was Promised Land, an unusual and intriguing French-Canadian and Italian production, in which the main character is a rock.

With the eloquent use of creative movement and non-verbal communication, the play depicts the story of the rock and it's interaction with humanity, from prehistoric to post modern times.

The actors' elaboration demonstrates the rocks permanence and strength through changing times. The rocks stability entices us to remember that it is on rock, not sand, that we should build our own foundation for greater emotional balance.

When we depend on something more durable, solid and timeless than even a rock, we depend on the everlasting strength of a higher power.

When we depend on a higher power, we depend on prayer.

During difficult times, when we pray, it often leads to a greater awareness and a stronger bond with a higher power, even during times of peace.

We are on a road to a point in time, and to a place in history, in which spiritual energy is very intense. All we need to do is ask for help from a higher power, and help will be given.

Still, many people reject the notion of prayer and a higher power. Some pray, but only for themselves. Others pray, but not often and not from the heart.

John Bunyan says, "In prayer it is better to have a heart without words than words without a heart."

We need not wait for the right words, place or time. If the only prayer we say is a heartfelt word of thanks, that will be the right word, place and time.

Build your house on rock. Invite the divine into your life through prayer. Once you have asked, with earnestness and sincerity, doubting nothing, prayers will be answered. Assume that whatever you ask for in prayer, you have already received.

And if you still need a reason to pray, pray for guidance. Pray for a strong and sensitive heart. Pray to become a better person. Pray not for the end to problems, but for the ability to handle them. Ask that you receive knowledge of all that you need to give. Pray to do the will of God in every situation. Ask to be granted divine wisdom and spiritual insight.

Ask simply for blessings, and know that you will get what is best for you.

Food for thought:
"I said a prayer for you today
And know God must have heard -
I felt the answer in my heart
Although He spoke no word!
I didn't ask for wealth or fame
(I knew you wouldn't mind) -
I asked Him to send treasures
Of a far more lasting kind!
I asked that He'd be near you
At the start of each new day
To grant you health and blessings
And friends to share your way!
I asked for happiness for you
In all things great and small -
But it was for His loving care,
I prayed the most of all!"
Source Unknown

Pray!

Date & Pecan Oatmeal
Cookies & Considerations
on following page.

Date & Pecan Oatmeal Cookies

4 cups flour
2 tsp. baking soda
1 tsp. baking powder
2 tsp. salt
2 cups butter
2 cups sugar
2 cups brown sugar
4 eggs
1 tsp. vanilla
5 cups rolled oats
2 cups toasted pecans
12 oz. (2 cups) chopped dates

Combine flour, baking soda, baking powder, and salt. Set aside. Cream butter and sugars well. Add eggs and vanilla. Add dry ingredients and rolled oats. Add pecans and dates. Drop onto cookie sheets.

Bake at 350 for 12 minutes.

Cookies & Considerations:

There is a special place for prayer. That place is within.
There is a special time for prayer. That time is anytime.

Make a date with a prayer. Make these Date & Pecan Cookies and pray that those who enjoy them when they're done will taste the love you make them with.

Lemon Oatmeal Cookies

1 & 1/2 cups whole-wheat flour
1 Tbsp. mace
4 tsp. baking powder
1 tsp. baking soda
1/2 tsp. salt
3 cups oats
1 cup butter
1 cup sugar
1/2 cup brown sugar
2 eggs
1 tsp. lemon extract
1 cup pecans

Combine flour, mace, baking powder, baking soda, salt and oats. Set aside. Cream butter and sugars. Add eggs and extract, beating well. Add flour mixture and pecans and blend thoroughly. Form into balls and flatten slightly. (Dough will be stiff.)

Bake at 350 for 10 - 12 minutes.

Cookies & Considerations:

This is one of my favorite oatmeal cookies. The subtle flavors of lemon and mace are enough to make it a unique and hearty, crispy, chewy, oatmeal cookie.

I Know I Am, But What Are You?!

Back home, when I was 9 or 10, we lived in a trailer park.

In that trailer park, I broke my arm, learnt to ride a bike, and I swung on the swings with my sister, singing "Old Pappy's Whiskers" and "Do Your Ears Hang Low" at the top of my lungs.

In that trailer park, there lived a handsome older boy named Randy. For some reason, the kids in the neighborhood took it as their duty, for a brief period of time, to taunt and torment Randy with name calling and hurtful words.

One day, while watching and listening from the sidelines, a clear voice spoke loudly above the din. "His name is Randy," it simply said and all heads turned.

Maybe it was the shock of hearing a normally quiet, shy girl dare to speak out. Maybe it was just boring enough or time to pick on someone else. Whatever it was, it was enough to stop the name calling.

Randy soon moved on, but the picture of that moment remains vivid in my mind. I had no prior knowledge that there existed, in me, the voice with which to speak the words that leapt out unchecked.

Admittedly, I'd participated - not by doing the name calling, but by not speaking out sooner.

My silence spoke volumes.

Not speaking out against bullying is wrong because children who bully and do not learn to deal appropriately with their conflicts, grow up to be adults who bully - the adults that many of us encounter at work and at play, sometimes even in our own families.

We need to teach children how to overcome obstacles without intimidation or browbeating. Unfortunately, when our children go to school to learn, one of the most difficult lessons they are taught has nothing to do with the three R's. Their encounters with bullies teach lessons of pain and misery, heartache and suffering. They must learn how to pretend that words don't hurt, that abuse and insults don't matter and that mean and nasty jokes are irrelevant. Hearts close and walls go up.

Bullies discriminate against others who are different. The differences may be appearance, race or religion; they may be Jews, blacks, gays, ethnic Albanians or Serbs.

To suggest that the crisis in Kosovo is the result of bullying may seem significantly understated but bullies cause war. It is caused by people who have never learnt to resolve their problems other than with hate.

Just as childhood bullying may sometimes be ousted as "normal play", so might the actions of Yugoslav President, Slobodan Milosevic, be dismissed as ethnic cleansing. But we aren't talking about a bubble bath here, are we?

Belittle the effects of bullying on the playground and you might belittle and underestimate the ravages and horrors of war. War, like bullying, starts with hurtful intent.

Speak out about it.

In the war against hatred, silence is not golden.

When silence is practiced in the face of hatred, we become an integral part of the problem.

If you think it has nothing to do with you, you're wrong.

Food for thought:
"You can bear this warning voice to generations yet to come. I look upon war with horror."
William Tecumseh Sherman (1820-1891)

Speak!

Chocolate, Macadamia & Espresso Biscotti
Cookies & Considerations
on following page.

Chocolate Macadamia & Espresso Biscotti

5 & 1/2 cups flour
5 tsp. baking powder
2/3 cup cocoa powder
1 tsp. salt
1 Tbsp. instant espresso powder
(or substitute 2 Tbsp. instant coffee dissolved in 1 tsp. water)
1 cup butter
2 cups sugar
6 eggs
1 cup semisweet chocolate chips or chunks
1 cup coarsely chopped macadamia nuts
1 egg white
extra sugar
melted white chocolate for dipping (optional)

Combine flour, baking powder, cocoa powder and salt. Set aside. Cream butter. Add sugar and beat till combined. Beat in eggs and espresso powder. Add flour mixture. Stir in chocolate and nuts. Divide dough into 4 pieces. Shape each piece into an 11" log and, on a cookie sheet, flatten to 2 & 1/2" wide. Combine egg white with 1 tsp. water. Brush on logs and sprinkle with sugar.

Bake at 350 for 25 minutes. Cool 1 hour. Slice diagonally into 1/2" slices, and bake again at 325 for 15 minutes. Cool & dip in melted white chocolate.

Cookies & Considerations:

If it were as simple as sitting down and talking over a cookie and a glass of milk, I'd deliver it personally.

But this might take more than a cookie and a glass of milk.

Maybe it will take compassion, forgiveness, awareness, willingness, respect, morality, and even a bit of humor and whole lot of love, courage and understanding to be able to see that we can get along, if we will only allow it.

Despite the different colors, flavors and textures, these crackle topped cookies get along well with just about anything. They'll mail well to bullies, and to people being bullied, anywhere in the world.

Chocolate, Chocolate Chunk Walnut Cookies

4 & 1/4 cups flour
1 cup cocoa powder
2 tsp. baking soda
2 tsp. salt
2 cups butter
1 1/2 cups white sugar
1 1/2 cups brown sugar
2 tsp. vanilla
4 eggs
12 oz. (or a 300 gram package) semi-sweet chocolate chips or chunks
1 1/2 cups walnuts

Combine flour, cocoa powder, baking soda, and salt. Set aside. Cream butter and sugars. Add vanilla and eggs, beating till creamy. Gradually add flour mixture. Stir in chocolate and walnuts. Drop onto cookie sheets.
Bake at 350 for 9 - 11 minutes or till done.

Cookies & Considerations:
This is one of my favorite chocolate cookie recipes. The chocolate flavor is doubled for those days when you need a double-dose of chocolate, and if you don't overbake them, it's like eating a brownie.

"Fear less, hope more;
Whine less, breathe more;
Talk less, say more;
Hate less, love more;
And all good things are yours."
Swedish Proverb

Life is Like a Game of Basketball

Sometimes, it seems to me, life is like a game of basketball.

Historians agree that basketball was invented by James Naismith in 1891. Canadians claim he was Canadian. Americans claim he was American. (What could be more like real life?!)

Wherever he was from, he wanted to invent a winter sport that could be enjoyed indoors, during the winter months, with no tackling or violence, and using skill instead of force.

The fundamental principles of basketball have stood the test of time. While moves have been perfected, style and performance have changed the look. Through it all, old fashioned ideals have been preserved. Life? Same.

On the court there are players, each with different positions and purposes. There are referees to arbitrate, umpires to mediate, and scorekeepers to placate. Playing floor sizes and markings vary. At each end of the court is a basket or goal. Life? Same.

The basic skills for basketball combine an intricate blend of timing, intuition and cooperation. Life? Same.

Penalties are given for violations and fouls. Double dribbling, pushing, pulling, bumping, holding, tripping and charging are all infractions of the rules in the game of basketball. There are common fouls, double fouls, multiple fouls and player controlled fouls. While some of life's fouls differ, pushing, pulling, bumping, holding, tripping and charging are generally frowned upon. So, life? Same.

The game is played with one side choosing baskets for the start of the game. The teams change baskets at half time. In life, many of us would do well to experience both sides of an issue before casting judgment. In the name of fair play, perhaps it would give us the ability to see and understand more clearly and with greater compassion. So, life? Same.

Even basketball terms relate to real life. An air ball is a shot that completely misses the rim and the backboard. An alley-oop shot is made by a player who leaps high to catch a pass lobbed by another player. The ball is then dropped or thrown into the basket before the player lands. An assist is a pass to a teammate who then scores. A blind pass is a pass made by a player to a teammate without looking at the teammate. Pivot foot is when a player, who is holding the ball, keeps a stationary foot while pivoting. Rebound is the recovery of a shot that bounces off the backboard or the rim. Screen or pick is the maneuver of an offensive player who hopes to free a teammate from the guard of a defensive player by setting himself in the path of the defender. Traveling is a violation that occurs when a player in possession of the ball takes more than one step or moves his pivot foot without dribbling.

Traveling is also when you pack your suit case and go to Mexico or someplace warm and exotic to lie on a the beach. Life?

Life is a team sport.

Life is not a spectator sport.

Someone get the ball!!

Food for thought:
"All I can do is play the game the way the cards fall."
James A. Mitchener

Participate!

Rum-Currant Shortbread
Cookies & Considerations
on following page.

Rum-Currant Shortbread

1/2 cup rum
1 cup currants
1 tsp. vanilla
2 cups flour
1/2 tsp. salt
1 cup butter
2/3 cup icing sugar
sugar for rolling

Heat rum. Add currants and vanilla and let stand till rum is absorbed (about an hour). Meanwhile, combine flour and salt. Set aside. Whip butter till fluffy. Add icing sugar. Add flour mixture and beat till well mixed. Add currants. Shape cookies into balls. Roll in sugar and place on cookie sheet. Flatten slightly with a potato masher or cookie press.

Bake at 350 for 12 - 14 minutes or till light golden!

Cookies & Considerations:

Sky hooks, finger rolls, slam dunks, and hang time. That's almost what it took, but a friend of a friend managed to replenish my exhausted supply of the finest Mexican vanilla, which really accentuates the marvelous flavor of these cookies. And the alcohol cooks out of them, so they're okay for basketball players of all ages.

"Love is a game that everyone can play and win."
Cecilia Lortscher

Gingerbread Men

2 & 1/2 cups flour
1 & 1/2 tsp. baking soda
1/2 tsp. salt
1 & 1/2 tsp. cinnamon
1 & 1/2 tsp. ginger
1/2 tsp. cloves
1/2 tsp. allspice
1/2 tsp. nutmeg
1/2 cup butter or margarine
1/2 cup brown sugar
1/2 cup molasses
1 egg

Combine flour, baking soda, salt and spices. Set aside. Cream butter and brown sugar. Add molasses and egg and blend well. Add flour mixture and cream till mixed. Dust work surface with flour and roll out dough to 1/4" thick. Cut with cookie cutters. Brush with beaten egg, decorate and bake or bake, then ice and decorate afterwards.

Bake for 8 - 10 minutes at 350 or till done.

Cookies & Considerations:

Miracles are for those who believe in the magic of a Gingerbread Man. Believe that you can eat a Gingerbread Man (head first, feet and legs first, or hands and arms first) and he will still live on, tickling your tummy with his lively two-step, and serenading you with his silent songs of love.

Life is a Paradox

I know a man who, without over-generalizing, is a somewhat typical male from his life span and background. He never said much and didn't get very involved in the day to day running of the household. He viewed himself as the bread earner, feeling that it was his job to take care of the family's basic material needs.

He never had much interaction with his kids while they were growing up. Putting great value in having a male heir, meant that his daughters learnt to understand that whatever time he did rarely spend with his children, he would favor his only son.

But, life being life, things don't always work out the way we think they will. So it was, the day that man's son took his own life.

Only afterwards, did that man do something for the very first time in his life. I was amazed to hear him say words I had never heard from him.

What a remarkable lessons those words were for me then, and how much they continue to teach me. Many years later, I still appreciate what a great price it cost for that man to be able to say "I love you".

Thanks, Dad. I love you, too.

Suicide, it is said, is a permanent solution to a temporary problem.

For reasons that are often never fully understood, some people choose to end their own lives. Friends and family are obligated to make some sense of the inescapable questions with no answers. There is inevitable speculation of what could have been done, now that hindsight has granted perfect vision. Misplaced feelings of guilt take up residence.

There is a stigma surrounding the occurrence of suicide. The subject is often taboo, off limits for fear that the mere mention of it will cause someone to consider it an answer to their problems. Of course, studies have shown that this is not true. In part, the prevention of suicide involves realizing that old attitudes must give way to acceptance of a problem that needs to be dealt with frankly and openly.

Because there are no ironclad rules, understanding suicide is no easy feat. There are many anomalies and exemptions. Though the motives for suicide are deep and long standing, suicide is actually not about death, but about ending a hopeless sense of pain. A greater awareness will rid us of the misconceptions and myths surrounding suicide.

A friend who sees the danger signs, who can talk openly and candidly, is also someone who will take the initiative to see that help is obtained.

Early recognition of the warning signs (even in ourselves) and proper treatment of mental disorders are the best deterrents.

Knowing that problems are only temporary, helps. Knowing that there are choices, helps. Knowing there is someone you can talk, who cares and understands, helps. Reading helps. Coping with grief helps. Faith helps.

Opening our hearts to care, our minds to see, our mouths to speak, our ears to listen and our arms to embrace, helps.

The recovery process begins slowly, by scratching away at the darkness. One day at a time, you pick at it. As the first crack opens, it lets in a bit of light. Daily, a bit more light comes, until one day, there is enough light, and hope, that we leave the darkness, and promise to go on.

And that, I believe, is essentially what the darkness is supposed to teach - that it has to get dark out before we can see the stars.

Food for thought:
"Yesterday is history. Tomorrow is a mystery. Today is a gift. That's why we call it the present."
Author Unknown

Twinkle!

Shortbread Cutouts
Cookies & Considerations
on following page.

Shortbread Cutouts

1 pound butter
1/2 cup berry sugar
3 cups flour

Cream butter. Mix in sugar. Add flour. Whip till well blended. Roll on floured surface and cut into trains and other shapes.
Bake at 325 for 12 - 15 minutes.

Cookies & Considerations:

My dad likes shortbread in the shape of a train. Baking cookies for someone you love, is a great way to say "Happy Father's Day, Dad! Love is everywhere, and I love you."

"I'll paint you a rainbow to hang on the wall,
to brighten your heart when the grey shadows fall.
On a canvas of joy outlasting the years,
with a soft brush of sweetness to dry all your tears.
I'll paint you a rainbow with colors of smiles
That glow with sincerity over the miles.
On a palette of words I will tenderly blend
Tones into treasures of sunlight and wind.
I'll paint you a rainbow that reaches so wide,
Your sights and your sorrows will vanish inside,
And deep in the center of each different hue,
A memory fashioned especially for you.
So lift up your eyes, for suspended above,
A rainbow designed by the fingers of love..."
"I'll Paint You A Rainbow," by Grace E. Easley

Hazelnut Meringues

2 egg whites
1 cup sugar
1 & 1/2 cups toasted, ground hazelnuts

milk chocolate for drizzling, if desired

Beat egg whites till foamy. Gradually add sugar and continue beating till stiff peaks form. Fold in hazelnuts. Drop onto parchment lined baking sheet.

Bake ate 300 for 15 - 20 minutes, or till firm and dry, but not brown. Drizzle with melted chocolate.

Cookies & Considerations:

(This recipe originally went with a column about music. See if you can tell?)

A favorite at our house, these cookies really rock! They're enjoyable with a quiet cappuccino, while conducting the orchestra, beating the drums, or strumming the guitar. They're even fancy enough to take to the next concert you give or recital you attend.

"Learning music by reading about it is like making love by mail."
Luciano Pavarotti

Laughter is Medicine for the Heart

The Consort Hospital sent me a fax a few days ago. (Odd, since I've never been anywhere near the Consort Hospital.)

The fax was titled "How to Handle Stress". It had a list of 30 short and humorous ways to relieve the stress in our lives. From the list of 30, my top ten picks, are:

#10.) Drive to work in reverse.

#9.) Make up a language and ask people for directions.

#8.) Use your Mastercard to pay your Visa.

#7.) Start a nasty rumor and see if you recognize it when it comes back to you.

#6.) Jam 39 tiny marshmallows up your nose and try to sneeze them out.

#5.) Stare at people through the tines of a fork and pretend that they're in jail.

#4.) Read the dictionary upside down and look for secret messages.

#3.) Write a short story using alphabet soup.

#2.) Make a list of things to do that you've already done.

#1.) When someone says "Have a nice day" tell them you have other plans.

I'm not even sure where Consort is, but when I've sufficiently reduced the stress in my life, I will go and look it up on a map. Of course, we don't recommend that you actually try many of these. (I'm especially worried about #6. My brother tried it with cherry pits and it was not a good thing!)

A sense of humor, and the ability to laugh at ourselves, is a priceless tool for beating stress. At any stage of our lives, a touch of humor, and a bit of laughter, can bring about optimism, diffuse difficulties, ease frustrations, change our sense of perspective and reduce stress. In hectic daily schedules, a touch of humor jump starts the soul, opens our hearts and reminds us that we are, after all, human.

Art Linkletter knew that children are especially helpful in putting the humor back in our lives. They really do say the darndest things, and they usually have the ability to bring laughter to our otherwise dull and crabby days. They remind us how to laugh at ourselves.

This summer, a little girl colored my day by telling me how much she liked to watch "those little beavers". The "little beavers" she was referring to were, in fact, big, plump gophers whose round bellies had been so copiously well fed that they were dragging bottom!

Not with hurtful jokes, not with nasty tricks, but with grace, laughter can enlighten and soothe. Like a fall breeze, it can cleanse, cool and refresh. Laughter can help keep our worlds from collapsing.

Any way we can find to bring more humor into our lives will lighten our hearts. Laugh easily, naturally, and spontaneously because unbridled laughter is medicine for your heart.

Laughter, like a smile, is the same in any language. As seen on a bumper sticker in Banff, where so many languages converge, "Please, not so close - we hardly know each other."

Food for thought:
"Laughter is the brush that sweeps away the cobwebs of the heart."
Mort Walker

Smile!

Peanut Butter Trail Mix
Cookies & Considerations
on following page.

Peanut Butter Trail Mix Cookies

4 & 1/2 cups rolled oats
1/4 cup whole wheat flour
2 tsp. baking soda
1/2 tsp. salt
1/2 cup butter
1 & 1/2 cups peanut butter
1 cup sugar
1 cup brown sugar
2 tsp. vanilla
3 eggs
1 & 1/2 cups trail mix

Combine oats, flour, baking soda and salt. Set aside. Cream butter and peanut butter with sugar and brown sugar until light and fluffy. Add vanilla and eggs. Blend well and stir in trail mix. Drop onto cookie sheets. Smish em down a little bit.
Bake at 350 for 12 minutes or till golden.

Cookies & Considerations:
At Costco on a Saturday afternoon, one man remarked, "I had to park so far away, I'm in another date line!" (I would have said "time zone" but they both work.)
Whether you make your own trail mix or buy it at Costco, both or neither, these almost flour-less, high protein, high fiber cookies are good for the heart, and they're yummy too. Take two, with a hearty laugh, and call the doctor in the morning if you don't feel better.

Molasses Crinkles Chews

4 & 1/2 cups flour
4 tsp. baking soda
2 tsp. cinnamon
4 tsp. ginger
1 tsp. cloves
1 tsp. nutmeg
1 tsp. allspice
1/2 tsp. salt
1 cup butter or margarine
1/2 cup shortening
2 cups brown sugar
1/2 cup molasses
2 eggs

cinnamon sugar for rolling

Combine flour, baking soda, cinnamon, ginger, cloves, nutmeg, allspice and salt. Set aside. Cream butter or margarine and shortening with brown sugar. Add molasses and eggs. Stir in flour mixture. Mix well. Shape into balls, roll in sugar or cinnamon sugar and drop onto cookie sheets.

Bake at 350 for 10 - 12 minutes or till just set.

Cookies & Considerations:

These heartily spiced cookies are one of my favorites. Crispy & chewy, they're great anytime, but especially so with a cup of tea or a glass of milk.

Kindness is a Chain - Pass It On!

"You don't owe me a thing. I've been there too. Someone once helped me out, the way I'm helping you. If you really want to pay me back, here's what you do. Don't let the chain of love end with you."

That quote is from "The Chain of Love", a true story, portrayed in a song, told by Jonnie Barnett and Rory Lee, to Chicken Soup for the Country Soul.

Being of a giving nature, we sometimes do favors for no reason other than to be of service. Basic kindness is the joy of giving with a generous heart and expecting nothing in return - not even a thank you.

Though they are unparalleled when passed on anonymously, spontaneously and randomly, any act of kindness has the ability to boost an ego, dispel a fear, shatter differences and brighten a day. Every time we share a kindness, warmth penetrates hearts and lifts them - even our own.

With our kind hearts, we show compassion.

With our kind words, we show respect and instill peace and contentment.

With our kind deeds we renew faith and hope.

Unexpected and purely given, the lasting impression of a kind gesture, just because we care, can bring as much joy to the giver as to the recipient.

When we are recipients of acts of kindness, we gladly fulfill an conscious obligation to continue the chain of love by performing small courtesies for others.

Whether they are small and quiet or large and loud does not matter at all. Although our small acts of kindness may sometimes seem insignificant, we never know how far they will reach, who they will benefit, or what series of other kind acts they may set off. Our generosity will often go a great deal further than the person we give it to.

Kindness is a strong and powerful chain. We are all links in the kindness chain and love is what holds the links together. Don't let the chain of love end with you - keep it unbroken. By granting kindness we add our own links to the chain and "pass it on".

Food for thought:
"When we cast our bread upon the waters, we can presume that someone downstream whose face we will never know will benefit from our action, as we who are downstream from another will profit from that grantor's gifts."
Maya Angelou

Link!

Kindness
Cookies & Considerations
on following page.

Kindness Cookies

1 & 1/2 cups flour
1 tsp. baking soda
1 tsp. salt
1 cup butter
1 cup sugar
1 cup brown sugar
2 eggs
1 tsp. vanilla
3 cups rolled oats
1 cup chopped, toasted hazelnuts
1 cup chopped, dried apricots
1 cup milk chocolate chips

Combine flour, baking soda and salt. Set aside. Cream butter and sugars. Add eggs and vanilla, blending well. Add flour mixture and rolled oats and mix till combined. Add hazelnuts, apricots and chocolate chips. Drop onto baking sheets and flatten slightly.

Bake at 350 for 12 minutes, or till golden brown.

Cookies & Considerations:

Getting my car stuck in the snow gave me the opportunity to remember to appreciate the simple kindness of others first hand. (Ironically, I used the same car the very next day, to pass on the kindness by taking someone, who had been locked out of his home, downtown for a key and then back home.)

Our kind acts reflect who we are, and I know no reciprocity is required. The rewards of acts of kindness are the warm feelings of having done something humane, compassionate and charitable for someone.

However, kind acts should be thanked, rewarded and passed on. Cookies are a great way to express and demonstrate kindness. They're also a great way to reward and pass on kindness. These cookies are yummy and chewy with a tasty blends of some unique flavors - pass them and continue the chain.

Giant Oatmeal Chocolate Chip Cookies

3/4 cup flour
3/4 cup whole wheat flour
1 tsp. baking soda
1/2 tsp. salt
3 cups rolled oats
1/2 cup butter
1/2 cup shortening
1 cup sugar
1 cup brown sugar
2 eggs
1 tsp. vanilla
1 - 12 oz. bag milk chocolate chips
1 cup walnuts
cinnamon sugar for rolling

Combine flours, baking soda, salt and rolled oats. Set aside. Beat butter and sugars until light and fluffy. Add eggs and vanilla. Add flour mixture. Stir in chocolate chips and walnuts. With a spring loaded ice cream scoop, form dough into large rounded spoonfuls. Roll in cinnamon sugar and drop onto baking sheets. Flatten slightly.

Bake at 350 for 12 - 20 minutes (depending on size), or till golden.

Cookies & Considerations:

These easy to make cookies are full of fiber and other good things, and the cinnamon sugar on top gives them a "Mexican hot chocolate" taste.

Lost and Found

The fruits of my walk were bountiful on this day. I found a lucky penny (not worth much in the monetary sense, but I can't pass one by), a beer (full!!) and a denture.

Yup, I found a denture. It looks like an upper, and it's a bit dirty and now it has tissue on it, but it is a denture. So if you're missing yours, I think I might have it.

Although the penny was originally found afterwards and at an entirely different location altogether, the beer and the denture were found in more or less the same place. (Could that be a coincidence, I wonder!) I'm feeling strongly tempted to donate the penny to the owner of the denture. Obviously you need more and better luck than I do. Either that, or you could consider the penny my contribution towards something really sticky that will keep that thing (the denture) where it belongs.

I'm absolutely grateful to have found these items. (They gave me something to write about.) I'd be doubly delighted if the rightful owner got the denture back. I don't really care about the beer, and you can rest assured that I will not personally drink it. (The beer is, in fact, more revolting to me than the denture.) Although I find it easy to justify losing the beer and especially the penny, the denture is causing me some marvel. How could you not notice its absence? Not having dentures myself (thankfully) I'm not quite sure how such a thing could happen. I am, however, absolutely, positively, utterly, completely and entirely convinced that there is a really, really, really, good explanation.

Anyway, if they're yours and you're still looking for them (the penny, the beer or the denture) I would be unequivocally pleased to return them to your possession. Really! No questions asked out loud unless if I really can't help myself!

Food for thought:
"We must not, in trying to think about how we can make a big difference, ignore the small daily differences we can make which, over time, add up to big differences that we often cannot foresee."
Marian Wright Edelm

Rejoice!

Hermits

2 & 1/4 cups flour
1/2 tsp. baking powder
1/2 tsp. baking soda
2 tsp. cinnamon
1 tsp. nutmeg
1 tsp. ginger
1/2 tsp. mace
3/4 cup butter
1 & 1/2 cups brown sugar
2 eggs
2 tsp. vanilla
1 cup walnuts
1 cup raisins
1 cup chopped dates

Combine flour, baking powder, baking soda, cinnamon, nutmeg, ginger and mace. Set aside. Cream butter and brown sugar. Add eggs and vanilla extract. Beat till creamy. Add flour mixture. Blend thoroughly. Add walnuts, raisins and dates. Drop onto greased cookie sheets.

Bake at 350 for 10 minutes, or till light brown on edges.

Cookies & Considerations:

Here's a recipe for Hermits, which is what you'll be if you don't get your teeth back.

Listen to Your Dreams

One of my newest best friends is going through a rough time. Her daughter is battling breast cancer for the second time. October is breast cancer awareness month, but even this month, we are very aware.

I'm reminded of a powerful dream once I had.

I was talking to my mother. She was shirtless and had her bare back to me. As she turned, I saw that she had no breasts. I then realized in my dream I was not talking to my mother but to my grandmother. Peculiar, because I never met my grandmother, or even seen pictures of her. Upon waking, the dream remained vividly clear. Forgetting it was impossible.

I asked Mom about Grandma a few days later. Grandma had, evidently, lost both her breasts to cancer.

Since it was time for my yearly check up, I mentioned to my doctor that there was a history of breast cancer in the family. Neither of us could feel a lump. Together, we decided that I should go for a mammogram, even though I was younger than the usual recommended age for regular mammograms. As it turned out, there was a lump that the doctors couldn't identify as "good" or "bad". Since it didn't belong there, doing nothing was not a choice for me. I'll spare you the details, but the end result is, I'm tremendously grateful it was not cancer. I'm also grateful for a dream, and a forewarning from a wonderful woman I never had a chance to meet in person. Thanks Grandma.

According to statistics, this year, in North America alone, one in eight women will get breast cancer. Every 12 minutes a woman will die from breast cancer. In North America, it is the number one killer of women aged 35 to 54. Early detection and intervention are the best ways to reduce mortality rates, but still the rate of mortality is on the rise.

Sometimes the courses we're given, are lessons we'd rather drop out of. Try hard to embrace life's challenges. Look upon each day as an incredible gift and bless your situation. Get a regular check up, and don't ever let anyone send you home to keep an eye on it! Please, please, insist on being tested. This is one instance where "I don't want to know!" never applies.

For my newest best friend, if you can't help it, don't worry about it. You will make it through this. When you're discouraged and can see no way out, remember who you have by your side, walking with you through the day.

Food for thought:
"There is nothing the body suffers which the soul may not profit by."
George Meredith

Insist!

Chewy Chocolate Mint Cream Cheese Cookies

2 & 1/4 cups flour
1 & 1/2 tsp. baking soda
1 - 300 gram package mint chocolate chips, divided
1 - 250 gram pkg. cream cheese
1/2 cup butter
1 & 1/2 cups sugar
1 egg
extra chocolate for drizzling

Combine flour and baking soda. Melt 1 cup of chocolate chips. Set aside. Cream butter and cream cheese. Add sugar then egg. Mix till light and fluffy. Add melted chocolate. Add flour mixture and remaining chips. Drop onto cookie sheets.

Bake at 350 for 10 - 12 minutes. If desired, drizzle with additional melted chocolate.

Cookies & Considerations:
These cookies are favorites of another friend, who is a breast cancer survivor. She's been waiting patiently for this recipe, so these are especially for her, with my love. Make them for a special celebration, like the arrival of another absolutely glorious day.

"As we advance in life it becomes more and more difficult, but in fighting the difficulties the inmost strength of the heart is developed."
Vincent Van Gogh

Ordinary Heroes

All over the world, in every country, in every walk of life, within every race, every religion, every belief, in every size, shape and color - we find them. If we look for them everywhere that's where they'll be. There are no places without them. There are no rules about where to look and no wrong ways to search.

A young boy flees his homeland to escape the war zone that is his village.

A grandmother fights to keep her grandson.

An adult heals after surviving the Second World War as a Jewish child in occupied France.

Teens give up a part of their summer to fight for an end to child poverty.

A woman stands in line, waiting for food to be distributed, because sanctions against her country have created a short supply.

A handicapped youth endeavors to gain independence.

Past and present, they never go out of style. As role models, the good they do is generally contagious.

Our heroes are people who make us feel better for having seen, touched and known them. They may be people we know well or people we've never met. They are caring and nurturing, brave and admirable. Given a set of circumstances, they act with dignity, decency and compassion Heroes are true warriors with remarkable courage.

Heroes are people who keep giving and going. Heroes know they can do what they want because they have the bravado to follow their hearts. A hero finds the strength to go against peer pressure and controlling behavior. A hero is someone who would rather fight for principles than live up to them. A hero fights for what is right.

Sometimes, heroes are heroes because of what they don't do or say.

Not all athletes and winners are heroes. Not all sick people and people with disabilities are heroes. Not all children are heroes. Not all celebrities are heroes. Not all friends, mothers, fathers, sisters, or brothers are heroes.

Not everyone is a hero. But everyone can be a hero.

We don't create heroes, we treat ordinary people like human beings and they turn into heroes, even if it's just in our own eyes.

Ordinary people can be heroes. Ordinary heroes can change the world.

Food for thought:
"A boy doesn't have to go to war to be a hero; he can say he doesn't like pie when he sees there isn't enough to go around."
Ed Howe

Protect!

Molasses Oat Cookies

3 cup whole wheat flour
3 cups rolled oats
1 cup oat bran
1 Tbsp. baking soda
1 Tbsp. cinnamon
1 Tbsp. ginger
1 tsp. salt
1/2 tsp. cloves
1 1/2 cups oil
2 cups sugar
2 eggs
1/2 cup molasses
cinnamon sugar for rolling

Combine flour, rolled oats, oat bran, baking soda, cinnamon, ginger, salt, and cloves. Set aside. Combine oil, sugar, eggs and molasses. Stir in flour mixture. Shape dough into balls and roll in cinnamon sugar. Place on cookie sheets and flatten slightly.
Bake at 350 for 12 minutes.

Cookies & Considerations:
Make some cookies for your most beloved hero. It's a great way to say a big thank you.
These spicy, wholesome cookies will disappear so quickly, you'll have to be prepared to be a hero yourself. Just say you don't like them, when someone else wants the very last one.

Quiet And Solitude

Hello! Does anyone out there have time to read this? Or are you lost, overwhelmed, and wading, up to your armpits, through the swamps of complete and utter chaos?

Quick! Take the paper and run, don't walk, to the nearest bathroom. Lock yourself in. Turn the fan on (to obliterate outside noises - not inside ones). Find a place to sit. (I said S-I-T.) Get comfortable. Are you alone? Except for the fan, is it quiet? Good! Let's talk.

(Sometimes, the bathroom is the only place for a little break. Actually, some of my most inspirational and spiritual moments have occurred while locked in the bathroom with the fan on. Sometimes, it's the only place to find serenity.)

Serenity is the ability to find peace and quiet. Serenity is remaining calm while storm rages around you. Serenity is being the very essence of tranquillity while in the midst of battle. Serenity is the ability to live in, and enjoy, the present moment, with inner harmony and outer stillness, despite the pandemonium.

If you've ever had it, you'll notice its absence - sometimes yearning for it without knowing exactly what you're lacking. Often, it's lost by trying to simultaneously accomplish a multitude of tasks.

How often do you try to do more than one thing at a time? Are you distracted from a task one minute, only to be sidetracked by another, moments later? As difficult as it is to be focused on one thing when we're doing four, we sometimes begin sweating loudly well in advance of next week's commitments!

Are you feeling like a top that's about to spin into orbit? Don't run away from home! Ask yourself, "Of the four places I have to be on Wednesday evening, what's really important?". What are my priorities? What's most urgent?

Speaking of urgent, nobody leave the bathroom yet! Quiet and stillness will lead you to focus and tranquillity. I want you to be composed when you leave.

If you're physically, emotionally, or spiritually exhausted by the many directions and ways you have to squeeze to fit into your day, think about your choices - and don't come out of the bathroom until you've enjoyed a moment of stillness. Take a instant to review the collection of responsibilities on your plate, then choose to focus on what's most important right now.

And just before you unlock that door, remind yourself, lovingly and kindly, that you deserve, and can gracefully ask, that there be enough time to get everything done that you need to do. And there will be enough time.

Food for thought:
"We have only this moment, sparkling like a star in our hand. . . and melting like a snowflake. Let us use it before it is too late."
Marie Beynon Ray

Focus!

Framers' Cookies

1 & 3/4 cups flour
1/2 cup cocoa powder
1 tsp. baking powder
1 tsp. baking soda
1/2 tsp. salt
1 & 3/4 cups rolled oats
1 cup butter or margarine
1 cup white sugar
1 cup brown sugar
1 tsp. vanilla
2 eggs
cinnamon sugar for rolling

Combine flour, cocoa, baking powder, baking soda, salt, and rolled oats. Set aside. Cream butter and sugars. Add eggs and vanilla. Beat well. Add flour mixture. Blend thoroughly. Form balls and roll dough in cinnamon sugar. Place on cookie sheet.

Bake at 350 for 10 - 12 minutes.

Cookies & Considerations:
Focus on my newest invention, these chewy, chocolate-oatmeal cookies. Named by a framing crew, but you don't have to wear a belt and pack a pencil and a hammer to enjoy them!

In Good Hands

On the snowy sidewalk outside, lay a Bohemian Waxwing (or so I was later told).

I bent to gently pick it up. It was a beautifully elegant bird. Its delicate feathers are a velvety soft and silky smooth, brownish gray. A long, slender crest, a yellow tipped tail, and white, red and yellow wing tips added to its distinguishing features. He must have flown into a window, I thought.

I picked him up and decided to carry him for a while. He was either going to make it or not.

We went on my walk together. As I walked, he sat in my gloved hand, looking at me with his gorgeous, gloriously dark eyes. Soon, he tucked his head under and behind, into the crook of his wing and had 3 little bird-naps. While I walked, talked and prayed, he slept, woke and wiggling his toes. (Even in his sleep, he seemed to know just when I needed reassurance that he was still with me.)

I got all the way back home with Ruffles still in my hand. (My patting and the wind kept messing up his feathers, so he became "Ruffles".) What could I offer my new friend? Fruitcake? Shortbread? A cappuccino? Or water?

Instead of drinking, he pooped on my glove, spit out a huge whole berry and pooped again. He started to walk around on my hand, so I decided it was time to head outdoors again. I just got a few steps outside when to my joyful surprise, he flew off into a tree.

He rested there a few hours before finally moving on. I'm sure I saw him later with many of his friends.

How delightful that I was able to share my walk with such a beautiful creature. His trust in me was a small wonder. Holding him in the palm of my hand, I was enthralled at the astounding magnificence that he was able to bring to my day.

Yes, I thought, he certainly was in good hands, but they weren't mine.

Food for thought:
"Write it on your heart that every day is the best day in the year."
Ralph Waldo Emerson

Wonder!

Rolled Oat Cookies

3 cups quick-cooking oats
1 & 1/4 cups flour
1 tsp. salt
1/4 tsp. baking soda
1 cup butter
1 cup brown sugar
1/4 cup water
1 tsp. vanilla

Combine oats, flour, salt, and baking soda. Set aside. Cream butter and sugar. Add water and vanilla. Mix well. Add dry ingredients and mix well. Shape into 2 rolls (about 10 inches long). Wrap in waxed paper. Chill for 2 hours or overnight. Cut in 1/2" slices and place on greased baking sheets.

Bake at 350 for 12 minutes or till well browned

Cookies & Considerations:

Don't you just love a big hunk of a solid, oatmeal cookie? These slice and bake cookies have no raisins, no nuts, no chocolate, and no spices. Just butter and oatmeal, and a few other simple ingredients is all it takes to give this delectable, tasty, almost shortbread-like, cookie my vote. They're yummy.

Simply . . . Scratching Where it Itches

Lao-tzu recommends that we manifest plainness, embrace simplicity, reduce selfishness, and have few desires. Ziggy says we should appreciate the here and now because it's only here now!

In fact, there is great value in keeping things simple and unassuming and we can comfortably do it, by living in the here and now.

We get up in the morning and go to bed at night. In between are the fillings that change the flavors of our days. We keep busy as best we can, hopefully with all the sensibility and order that our souls require.

Technology is supposed to make our lives simpler and easier but we're drowning in it. It's hard to e-mail kindness, humanity and consideration. How do you send a hug over the Internet? A touch on the arm, a pat on the back, a tear, a sigh, eyes that meet and show you care. Can those be appreciated when left on voice mail?

Most of us understand the dangers of nuclear testing, but what are the dangers of misunderstanding the simple things that are so abundant, and so often taken for granted. Aren't they the substances that give our lives depth and meaning?

We complicate life, when it is not complex. We are. At some point, life becomes so busy, that it prevents us from enjoying what we're working so hard to achieve. We over-schedule until we must be accountable for every moment, rushing from one activity to another. Trying to satisfy our insatiable appetites for more, bigger, better becomes an indomitable task that we could never possibly hope to meet. Simplicity is merely a scratch we can't itch - like a dog trying to scratch behind its ears.

There is much to be learnt from dogs. They eat, sleep, play and scratch where it itches. Dogs are not impressed with looks, bank accounts, or social status. They don't require material possessions. They live naturally and in the present moment. They love deeply, loyally and faithfully.

They aren't worried about what went wrong yesterday, what has to be done tomorrow, the mistakes they made in the past or the endless possibilities of the future. They know what we are still learning - that it's the most simple enjoyments that most greatly improve the quality of our lives and bring us the greatest pleasure, if only we take the time to appreciate and delight in their simplicity.

Sometimes, we lose sight of the sweet, simple things in life. We forget that our greatest achievements are the memories we create for ourselves, those that touch our hearts. The finest memories we create for others are the ones that touch their hearts.

In the name of making things a little less complicated, keep breathing, amuse yourself with what you truly love, learn your lines, sit still once in a while, scratch where it itches and remember - the ultimate is to enjoy love and life, and to love life.

Food for thought:
"I have a simple philosophy. Fill what's empty. Empty what's full. Scratch where it itches."
Alice Roosevelt Longworth

Scratch!

Doggie Delights
(For Doggies)

4 cups whole wheat flour
1/2 cup wheat germ
1 cup powdered milk
1/2 tsp. garlic powder
1/2 tsp. salt
3/4 cup margarine
2 eggs
2 Tbsp. molasses
1 cup water

Combine flour, wheat germ, powdered milk, garlic powder and salt. Cut in margarine. Add eggs, molasses and water. Blend thoroughly, then knead lightly to form a ball. Roll out to 1/4" thickness and cut into dog bone shapes. Place on greased cookie sheet.
Bake at 350 for 20 - 30 minutes.

Cookies & Considerations:
In honor of a love for my favorite, furry, four-legged friends, I present these doggie cookies - not for human consumption, but I guess if your tummy's empty, they would fill it up without doing too much harm!

Moving Misdemeanors -
Home Isn't (Necessarily) Where Your Stuff Is

When we left Canmore, in late October, two years ago, we were not only leaving our home of 15 years, we were also leaving the first place I ever knew I belonged - my cheeks had told me so!

The move we made was so life changing for me, that I used to look back and wonder how I could have missed the messages I must have been sent. Then I realized that maybe I hadn't missed them after all.

Maybe that was why it was so hard to camp there the summer before. I cried in the camper. Maybe that was why it was so hard to take my kids out of school. I cried at their teachers. Maybe that was why it was so hard to sign the papers on the sale of the house. I cried at the lawyers. Maybe that was why it was so hard to make that last drive from Calgary to Canmore. I cried at the landscape. Maybe that was why I had doubts. I cried at myself.

"What brought you here?" the cashier at the Petro Canada asked after I explained that I really could rent the videos. Even though my truck said I was still in Alberta, I knew that I had well and truly arrived, and I could prove it if I had to. Funny she should ask, though, since by that time, I had already begun to wonder myself.

"I haven't got a clue!" I replied, as a bewildered look found a home on my face. My "stuff" was all with me, but I definitely didn't feel like I was "home".

Since I couldn't find this life lesson written in my own personal agenda, I wondered if someone had inadvertently signed me up. I set about looking for an answer.

In my clue-less condition, I could not see that the universe was unfolding as it should. All I had to do was choose. Accept and go with or fight and go against.

I chose the latter and made the move one of the hardest things I've ever done.

I had made major moves before, so no one was more surprised than I, when this one settled itself in to be a big ol' challenge and an unimaginable opportunity to learn. I like to say that, for the ten months we were away, it took me three months to dig myself into an immense hole, three to climb back out, two months to build a fence (not around myself!), and two months to move back.

Acceptance and enjoyment of circumstances the way they are, living in, focusing on and appreciating the moment, and a deeper spiritual connection are just a few of the little lessons I learnt in those ten months.

Victim or victorious - we chose the outcome. Out of adversity, we may grow.

We're often surprised when negative situations have positive outcomes, and when dark times, bring light. Our lessons, whatever they are, are there to teach us. We never stop getting lessons, and we will repeat our lessons until we learn them.

If I had known beforehand, what the next ten months would hold, I might not have had the courage to go. Now, I know that whatever happened, should have.

Food for thought:
"I dance to the tune that is played."
Spanish Proverb

Dance!

ANZAC
Cookies & Considerations
on following page.

ANZAC Cookies

2 & 1/4 cups rolled oats
2 & 1/4 cups flour
2 cups coconut
1 cup butter
2 Tbsp. golden syrup
1 & 1/4 cup sugar
2 tsp. baking soda
6 Tbsp. water

Combine rolled oats, flour and coconut. Set aside. Melt butter and syrup together. Cool slightly and incorporate sugar. Dissolve soda in water and add. Stir in oats and flour mixture. Form into balls, drop by spoonfuls onto greased cookie sheets and flatten slightly.

Bake at 350 for 8 - 10 minutes or till dark golden.

Cookies & Considerations:

Staying abroad, it was a wonderful surprise to get a fax from Patsy, many miles away, in New Zealand. Who better than me, to say the words in my heart, to Patsy, since she and I took small steps up the same mountain, but on different paths. Patsy's family and ours left town at about the same time, forever, lock, stock and barrel. Contrary to the song, Patsy, once you leave, you can always come back and I'm here to prove it. I continue to dream about starting a club in the valley for all the people who do just that - leave and come back, some more than once!

Patsy sent a couple of traditional recipes from New Zealand, including this one. I had seen the recipe before and wondered if Anzac was some sort of an unusual and exotic ingredient from the islands of Oceania. Another lesson learnt, since it turns out that ANZAC stands for Australia/New Zealand Army Corps and these cookies were made to send to soldiers during World War I. I also learnt that these cookies are very different, easy to mix, and very yummy. (I have already adjusted them for our slightly higher altitude. It is a stiff dough, but if yours is still too crumbly add 1 or 2 more tsp. of water.)

Sincere thanks for the history lesson, the encouragement and the recipes, Patsy. I do understand and I hope that makes a difference to you. You may be far away in New Zealand, but we can feel pieces of your heart here at "home". . .

Hazelnut Chip Cookies

2 & 1/2 cups rolled oats
2 cups flour
1 tsp. baking powder
1 tsp. baking soda
1/2 tsp. salt
12 oz. milk chocolate
1 cup toasted hazelnuts
1 cup butter
1 cup sugar
1 cup brown sugar
2 eggs
2 tsp. vanilla

In a food processor, blend oats to a coarse powder. Combine with flour, baking powder, baking soda and salt. Set aside. In food processor, coarsely grate chocolate. Set aside. In food processor, coarsely chop hazelnuts. Set aside with chocolate.

Cream butter and sugars. Add eggs and vanilla. Add flour-oat mixture. Add chocolate and nuts. Mix well. Roll into balls and flatten slightly.

Bake at 350 for 10 - 12 minutes, or till done.

Cookies & Considerations:

One of my favorite nuts, the hazelnut (also known as filberts) create a wonderfully unique taste. These cookies, from the crispy-chewy department, are crackle topped and loaded with chocolate.

Spaced Out Over Bear Bins

As Tommy would say on the Rugrats, "Hey, I gots a idea!"

I think we should see if we can have the Mir space station, and put our bear-proof garbage bins up there.

The way I see it, it's the only solution that makes any sense and here's why.

There are the obvious reasons: no one would be able see them from their kitchen/livingroom/bedroom, we wouldn't hear them or smell them, they wouldn't decrease anyone's property value, and (best of all) the bears would have a really hard time getting into them!

As well, we'd be doing the Russians a favor. Mir, the once upon a time advanced space station, is now a problem no one knows what to do with - not unlike our bear bins.

Since the Russians want to abandon ship, they probably don't care how much they get for it. In fact, mission control, in Korolyov, is probably, at this very moment, waiting for our recommendations on what to do with Mir.

I'm fairly certain they'd just give it to us, to be rid of their problem.

Instead of letting it blow itself out, we could use the outdated space contraption, along with my creative imagination and some duct tape, to make some minor modifications. The payoff would be a highly innovative, impromptu solution to all of our garbage woes.

Baring a sudden repeat of the onslaught of fires, crashes and thousands of other such emergencies (including the little nicks from meteorites and space debris), the old girl isn't looking too shabby. In fact, the space station has been running pretty good lately. First launched in February 1986, she's certainly held together (sort of) far longer than her 5 year expectancy.

Granted, she's high maintenance, but at $365 million Canadian, per year (that's $34.99 American), we could recoup some of the costs by manning it ourselves with volunteers - claustrophobics and neat freaks need not apply!

People could sign up for however long they wanted, but we could strongly encourage them to try to break the record held by cosmonaut Valeri Polyakov, who spend 438 consecutive days aboard Mir. (What on earth was he doing up there?!)

I digress. Equipped with a six-port docking section, Kelly and the other sanitary technicians could really haul. . . well, garbage. Bear bins and all, we could send the whole thing into orbit. And once we fill up Mir, we could just release our trash into outer space and see what happens when it re-enters the atmosphere.

Just in case, though, I think we should keep a few of the bear bins down here - probably in south Canmore. If the whole thing happens to accidentally re-enter the atmosphere, some of the 480,680 pounds of Mir that don't burn up or land in the Pacific Ocean might somehow make there way down here.

It would sure be nice to have someplace to put the extra pieces.

* * *

There's no doubt that the crews of Mir have learnt to tolerate their share of problems.

They've also learnt a lot about improvisation. Making do with what's at hand has become one of Mir's most significant lessons. Being able to spontaneously ad-lib a make shift solution has indicated to other space programs, that crew members should be trained to prepare for the unpreparable and rehearse for the unrehearsable.

Still, Mir's greatest lesson of improvisation may be yet to come. As it re-enters the atmosphere - controlled or uncontrolled - no doubt, we should expect the unexpected. Like our bear bins, there are many solutions - some are better than others.

Mir translates from Russian as "small autonomous community" or "peace". In the interest of maintaining peace in our small autonomous community, with a dash of global thinking, let us practice, not only the art of improvisation, but the art of tolerance.

Food for thought:
"Ask not that events should happen as you will, but let your will be that events should happen as they do, and you shall have peace."
Epictetus

Improvise!

Russia Tea Biscuits
Cookies & Considerations
on following page.

Russian Tea Biscuits

2 & 1/4 cups flour
1/4 tsp. salt
1 cup butter
3/4 cup icing sugar
1 tsp. vodka
3/4 cup ground hazelnuts
extra icing sugar

Combine flour and salt. Set aside. Cream butter and icing sugar. Beat in vodka. Slowly blend in flour mixture. Blend in hazelnuts. Roll dough into walnut-size balls and place on baking sheets. Flatten with the bottom of a glass dipped in flour.

Bake at 325 for 12 - 15 minutes or till light golden. Cool slightly and sprinkle with icing sugar.

Cookies & Considerations:

These hazelnut shortbread cookies might be too frangible to send into orbit, but they're sure tasty. No hazelnuts or vodka? Improvise!

"It is an indubitable fact that technological progress comes from God and, therefore, can and must lead to Him."
Pius XII Pacelli

Chocolate Chunk Pecan Cookies

5 & 1/4 cups flour
2 tsp. baking soda
2 tsp. salt
2 cups butter
1 & 1/2 cups white sugar
1 & 1/2 cups brown sugar
2 tsp. vanilla
4 eggs
12 oz. chocolate chunks (or chips)
1 & 1/2 cups pecans

Combine flour, baking soda, and salt. Set aside. Cream butter, and sugars. Add vanilla and eggs. Beat till creamy. Gradually beat in flour mixture. Stir in chocolate and pecans. Drop onto cookie sheets.

Bake at 350 for 10 - 12 minutes or till edges are golden brown.

Cookies & Considerations:

The cookie - and part of the column - that started it all!

Life is like a batch of cookies. Each ingredient contributes authentically to the whole, yet is ever changing and transforming what we have at any given moment. Such are the events in our lives - always changing and transforming. Instead of butter, sugar, eggs, chocolate and flour, consider the fires of your dreams, the sweat, the tears, your struggles and your passion for life are the ingredients. Go create your cookies, but promise me this. Be sure to enjoy the fragrance and the flavors you create and celebrate the perplexities that make your own recipe unique.

My, What Lovely Buns I Have

Thank you, Johnykins, for the "I love your buns" ad. You assist me in confessing, without a bit of vanity or embellishment, my belief that I have the very nicest buns in town! I know this to be the indisputable truth because I have been told it is so. (Sorry, Johnykins. You aren't actually the first to notice!) It is also my staunch belief that mine are the most talked about and sought after buns for miles around. Those who know might understand. It is therefore, my somewhat dubious honor, to bravely and confidently proclaim, right here and now, that my buns are plump and generally on the larger side.

Despite, or because, of that, I know that many of you would support me faithfully in my claim that my buns are practically irresistible. Oh, sure, there are other buns around. You've seen them - maybe you've even laid your hands them - but they aren't quite like mine!

Some buns can be much smaller, others tend to be not quite so well formed. Some buns are down right flat, but my buns are well rounded and have a delightful shape. When my delicious buns make an appearance, it's like sending an FTD bouquet - they make people happy all along the way!

Why, I have been told of the depths of eagerness and excitation that those most endearingly passionate about my luscious buns feel at having them so near. (Thanks, Johnykins!) I often blush at the great jubilation and joyous celebration that occurs whenever my buns arrive.

Yes, it's true. Having such lovely buns can be a bit of an embarrassment at times, but I try not to let it over inflate my already atrocious ego.

For those of you who haven't ever had the pleasure of getting up close and personal with my buns, I should explain myself before you look up the phone number for the Canmore Leader, intent on giving Carol Picard an earful. (I dare say that her ears are rarely "empty", but I would not like to be responsible for them being even more full than usual or necessary.)

Obviously, I have my tongue firmly planted in my left cheek, and, most likely, my right foot lodged solidly in my mouth. Oh, dear! Oh, well.

Clearly, both Johnykins and I speak, not of my buns that are attached approximately somewhere between my back and my legs, but of my tasty Cinnamon Buns, which he and a great many others are yearning for and hinting at (and not necessarily with great subtlety, I might add). Fear not, though, my loves. Those of you who are weak with hunger for my buns (and I especially mean you, Johnykins) may soon have your endless appetites somewhat appeased, although only temporarily, I'm sure. Your hearts may soon be swelling, much like my rising buns, at the thought that before long you will once again be able to reap my bounties. I'll keep you all posted - count on it!

As for you Johnykins, thank you for your boundless, hungry passions. Now, about those buns you love so much. . . if you give me a call, I'll arrange for you to get your hands on some!

Food for thought:
"What hunger is in relation to food, zest is in relation to life."
Bertrand Russell

Laugh!

Snickerdoodles
Cookies & Considerations
on following page.

Snickerdoodles

3 cups flour
1 tsp. baking soda
1/2 tsp. salt
1 tsp. cream of tartar
1/2 tsp. nutmeg
1 cup butter
1 & 1/3 cups sugar
2 tsp. vanilla
2 eggs

cinnamon sugar (1 cup sugar mixed with 1 Tbsp. cinnamon)

Combine flour, baking soda, salt, cream of tartar, and nutmeg. Mix together and set aside. Cream butter, sugar and vanilla till light and fluffy. Add eggs. Add the flour mixture. Mix till blended. Drop dough by rounded tablespoons into cinnamon sugar and roll.

Bake at 350 for 12 - 13 minutes. (Cookies will be firm and have cracks in the cinnamon sugar.)

Cookies & Considerations:

Since this is a cookie column, you don't get the recipe for my luscious cinnamon buns. (That's in the next book!) I had a few choices in mind for appropriate cookies. I thought that maybe Whoopee Cookies or some Half Moons might make an interesting finale, but settled for these classics, Snickerdoodles, a soft, chewy vanilla cookie, rolled in cinnamon sugar, in hopes that, not only will they do, but you'll remember to have a snicker or two now and then.

(These were my friend Patsy's favorites way back when.)

Kahlua Shortbread Cookies

2 & 1/4 cups flour
1/2 tsp. cinnamon
1/4 tsp. salt
4 tsp. Kahlua
1 tsp. instant coffee or espresso powder
1 cup butter
3/4 cup sugar
extra Kahlua and some ice

Combine flour, cinnamon and salt. Set aside. Combine Kahlua and coffee powder. Set aside. Cream butter with sugar. Add Kahlua. Gradually add flour mixture. Roll into balls and drop onto cookie sheet. Flatten with cookie press or bottom of glass.
Bake at 350 for 12 minutes.
(Pour extra Kahlua over ice and sip while cookies bake!)

Cookies & Considerations:
A delicate blend of strong flavors. The results? Taste for yourself.

"And it shall come to pass,
that before they call, I will answer . . .
and while they are speaking,
I will hear."
Isaiah 65:24

Once in a Blue Moon

Look up - look way up!

If it's clear out tomorrow you might see a blue moon.

Until January, when we had our first blue moon of the year, I never knew what one was. I'd heard the term "blue moon" and knew it had nothing to do with Gorgonzola, Limburger, Blue Cheese or any other kind of cheese. Nor did it, I presumed, refer to the color of the moon.

Live, learn, and pass it on. Simply put, a "blue moon" refers to the second full moon in one calendar month. Because our calendar is not attuned to the moon's 29 day cycle, we can expect a single blue moon to occur about once every 2.7 calendar years.

However, the last time there were two blue moons in one year, such as there are this year, was 1980. If you miss these ones, don't worry. In the calendar year 2018, there will be another two blue moons. The cycle for two blue moons in the same year repeats itself approximately every 19 years or, once in a blue moon.

Although the term "blue moon" has been around for more than 400 years, it isn't always associated with the occurrence of two full moons transpiring in one month.

Besides referring to a rarely occurring event (a term coined about 150 years ago), there have been times when particles in the air have made the moon actually appear to be blue. Dust from volcanic eruptions and smoke and ash from forest fires have seemed to turn the moon blue. But those events, too, come to pass only once in a blue moon.

If the blue moon has captured your rapture, you're not alone. The blue moon sets many minds to wondering.

Philosophers ponder life, the universe and the whole shebang.

Scientists give the blue moon high credits for resurrecting an interest in the natural wonders of the night sky.

Romanticist, Christopher Fry, has an interesting point of view. He blames the lecherous moon for a population increase. "The moon is nothing but a circumambulating aphrodisiac divinely subsidized to provoke the world into a rising birth-rate", he says.

Then there's Blue Moon, the song, by Rogers and Hart. With it's words of forlornness and despondency, it depicts the loneliness of a soul searching for it's mate.

So, go ahead, ponder the universe while you go for a romantic, moonlit walk. And when you get home, take out the binoculars and gaze at the moon in the night sky.

If the evening is clear and we take a moment to observe the beauty of the last blue moon of the century, we might speculate about life, the universe, romance, and the natural wonders of the gloaming sky.

We may also willingly marvel, wonder, and in all things see, that there is something sacred happening all around us.

We don't have to methodically interpret its existence. It can simply be - sweet sanctity!

Food for thought:
"Blue moon, you saw me standing alone, without a dream in my heart, without a love of my own. Blue moon, you knew just what I was there for, you heard me saying a prayer for, someone I really could care for."
Rogers & Hart

Wonder!

Moon Pies
Cookies & Considerations
on following page.

(Blue) Moon Pies

2 cups flour
1/2 cup cocoa
2 & 1/2 tsp. baking powder
1/2 tsp. salt
1/3 cup butter
1 cup sugar
1 egg
1 cup buttermilk
1 tsp. vanilla

Filling:
3/4 cup butter
1 cup icing sugar
1 tsp. vanilla
1/2 cup marshmallow topping

Combine flour, cocoa, baking powder and salt. Set aside. Cream together butter and sugar. Beat in egg. Add buttermilk and vanilla. Gradually add flour mixture. Drop by heaping tablespoons onto lightly greased or parchment lined baking sheets.

Bake at 350 for 8 - 10 minutes or until a toothpick tester comes clean. Cool.

For filling: Cream butter and icing sugar. Add vanilla then beat in marshmallow topping. To assemble, spread half the cookies generously with filling and top with remaining cookies, pressing together lightly.

Cookies & Considerations:

You might only make these cookies once in a blue moon, but whenever you do, you'll wonder why you don't make them more often.

Gazing at these cookies, you'll discover fun-filled moon balls of brown and white. The chocolate, cake-like cookie dough is baked, then sandwiched together with a creamy marshmallow filling.

They're natural wonders and may even lift feelings of forlornness and despondency and inspire romance and wonder. Hold the cheese!

If you don't have any buttermilk, make some sour milk by placing 1 Tbsp. of vinegar or lemon juice in a measuring cup and adding milk to make 1 cup. Let stand 5 minutes, then use as you would buttermilk.

Cowboy Cookies

2 cups flour
1/2 tsp. baking powder
1 tsp. baking soda
1 tsp. salt
2 cups rolled oats
1 cup sugar
1 cup brown sugar
1 cup butter
2 eggs
1/2 tsp. maple flavoring (or 1 tsp. vanilla)
1 - 12 oz. (300 gram) pkg. milk chocolate chips
1 cup walnuts

Combine flour, baking powder, baking soda, salt and rolled oats. Set aside. Cream butter. Add sugars. Mix well. Add eggs and vanilla. Add dry ingredients, followed by chocolate chips and walnuts. Drop onto cookie sheet.
Bake at 325 for 12 minutes.

Cookies & Considerations:

You don't have to be a cowboy or even anywhere near a cowboy (although it wouldn't hurt!), to bake and enjoy these Cowboy Cookies. They're yummy and a match made in heaven.

Okay, I'm Awake! Now Can I go Back to Sleep?

It's early. It's still dark. I'm awake! Now can I go back to sleep?

My mother never told me I'd feel like this, but then, she never was much of a "talker".

I still remember our "talk" when I first started menstruating. I took her into my bedroom, sat her on the bed beside me and told her. With an anxious and worried look on her face, she said, "You know what this is, don't you?"

I nodded a yes, and she left the room.

(That's the end of the story.)

My mother never told me I'd wait for my soul to wake up, only to have days when I'd rather pull the covers over my head, go back to sleep, and undergo life slumbering, unconscious, unaware.

It is said, by some, that our souls awaken at different times in our lives. Some of us are born with them alive, and some of us have gentler, more gradual awakenings. I believe my soul only began it's gentle, timid awakenings a few years ago. In that way, I suppose, I am a late bloomer.

The path to awakenings is, like many other paths, a long and pebbled road. It is a path laden with the challenges of hills and valleys, mountains and canyons. It is a path overflowing with my own needs and the needs of others, demands, chores and requests. It is a path teeming with the forks, branches and crossroads of decision and indecision. It is a path replete with the flowers of joy and the weeds of sorrow and misery.

Today, as my soul and I embark, once more, upon our journey, we will try to remember that our purpose is to manifest love, not hatred. We will attempt to demonstrate forgiveness, not condemnation. We will embody patience, not haste. We will exhibit empathy and display courage before we express indifference and dread.

My soul and I will endeavor to work quietly and consistently, without competition or grandstanding.

We will strive to overlook those who take our place in line. Instead, before they can take it, we will offer it to them.

Today, rather than complaining about a long wait, we will give thanks for a moment of stillness and quiet reflection.

When we see a beggar, a bully or a bigot, we will not question the fulfillment of their purpose, for that is something we do not know enough about.

By preference, we will open our hearts more readily, extend our assistance and relinquish compassion for their suffering.

On our path today, my soul and I will encounter people who have something to teach us. The same people will have something to learn from us.

We will be kind to the unkind, because perhaps if they have never seen it, they do not know the face of kindness.

As much as possible, my soul and I will choose to keep promises, to be gentle, to offer praise, and to give up the principle of right or wrong, good or bad - fully, freely, joyously.

As we awaken, we will bring to light a path that forever deepens and grows. It is a path based on knowledge and belief, but more importantly, it is a path based on knowledge acted upon and belief lived out and practiced. Even when it isn't convenient!

Soon, the sun will rise. As we sip our coffee, we hear the new day call our name. We won't roll over and go back to sleep - we're just waking up!

Food for thought:
"No matter how big or soft or warm your bed is, you still have to get out of it."
Grace Slick

Awaken!

Chocolate Raspberry Sandwiches
Cookies & Considerations
on following page.

Chocolate Raspberry Sandwiches

2 cups flour
1/2 cup cocoa
1/4 tsp. baking soda
1/4 tsp. salt
1 cup butter
3/4 cup icing sugar
1/2 cup sugar
1 tsp. vanilla
raspberry jam
extra chocolate for dipping or drizzling

Combine flour, cocoa, baking soda and salt. Set aside. Cream butter. Add sugars and vanilla and beat till light and fluffy. Add flour mixture and blend till combined and dough forms a ball. Between sheets of wax paper, roll out dough to 1/4" thickness. Cut with 2" cookie cutters. Place on cookie sheets.

Bake at 350 for 10 - 12 minutes. When cool, turn over half the cookies and spread with raspberry jam. Top with other cookies. Dip or drizzle with melted chocolate.

Cookies & Considerations:

When I woke up this morning, I didn't know that Desi would call to say that I had her "Jo-Jo, The Bird With Attitude". She might think I've been awakened from my slumber to find things. Maybe I have. I still have the doll I found, with the purple streak through her long blonde hair, but Desi's mom found the owner of the dentures.

I found this recipe for delicious, crispy, chocolate, sandwich cookies. Raspberry jam is tucked into chocolate shortbread and dipped in more chocolate. Mom never told me, but they're definitely worth waking up for!

Fig, Date and Walnut, Oatmeal Cookies

1 & 1/2 cups rolled oats
1/3 cup buttermilk
2 & 1/2 cups flour
1 tsp. baking powder
1 tsp. baking soda
1 tsp. cinnamon
1 tsp. nutmeg
1/2 tsp. salt
2 cups brown sugar
3/4 cup butter
2 eggs
1 tsp. vanilla
1/2 cup chopped figs
1/2 cup chopped dates
1 cup walnuts

Combine oats and buttermilk. Set aside. Combine flour baking powder, baking soda, cinnamon, nutmeg, and salt. Set aside. Beat together brown sugar and butter. Add eggs and vanilla. Stir in oat mixture. Beat in flour mixture. Add figs, dates and walnuts Roll in cinnamon sugar if desired. Drop onto greased cookie sheet.
Bake at 350 for 10 minutes or till golden.

Cookies & Considerations:
For the fig plucker . . . and the fig lover.

Remembering Who's in Charge

I believe that every event, every person and every circumstance, is sent into our lives with a divine intent (including that big, beautiful Raven, the size of an Emu, that just pooped on the deck rail - even if his only intent was to make me laugh!).

I believe that if we ask what we need to do, and if we watch and listen, we will be told.

I believe that not getting an answer, is an answer.

I believe that we'll know that we have the answer when we are at peace.

I believe that our answers sometimes come when we listen to, and act on, our intuition.

I believe someone's in charge, and it isn't me.

Let me tell you about Tia.

The day I met Tia, I had felt divinely impelled to walk a route I don't often chose. I wondered why.

When I met Tia, I knew she was the "why", but now I had to find out the "what".

At the time, she was heading in the opposite direction. Her well-planned day was snatched, without mercy, from the grasps of predictability, when she allowed herself the freedom to spontaneously change directions.

As we walked, Tia spoke and I listened, In the charming accent she'd acquired, years ago, from her origins in Hungary, she reminded me of many things, one being that, within the parameters of our journey, our set of circumstances, our ethnicity, our origins, we are all created equal.

She reminded me that we don't have to have different colored skin, to experience the effects of discrimination and racism. She reminded me that we can easily sense that, by being different, we are outsiders. She reminded me how profoundly our words and actions, that seem harmless, can cause harm to others. She reminded me that some wounds, inflicted by others, don't heal. Some wounds heal, but leave scares, like the ones she bears.

She spoke of the Golden Rule, which I remembered singing, with Yogi Bear's accompaniment. "Don't do unto others, what you don't want them to do, to you."

Tia was just what I needed. She reminded me to be open to the gifts the universe is willing to offer, like meeting her, as if by "chance".

　　She reminded me that, sometimes we should get out of the way, and let the one in charge, divinely intervene, while we carry on - with perfect timing, perfect grace and perfect knowledge. And with a heart full of faith.

Food for thought:
"Chance is always powerful. Let your hook be always cast. In the pool where you least expect it, will be a fish."
Ovid

Perceive!

Lemon Pine Nut Rounds
Cookies & Considerations
on following page.

Lemon Pine Nut Rounds

4 & 1/2 cups flour
2 tsp. baking soda
1/4 tsp. salt
1 cup butter
2 cups sugar
4 eggs
1 tsp. vanilla
1/2 cup lemon juice
1 Tbsp. grated lemon zest
1 cup pine nuts, finely chopped
extra sugar for rolling

Combine flour, baking soda, and salt. Set aside. Cream butter and sugar. Add eggs one at a time. Add vanilla, lemon juice, and lemon zest. Add flour mixture and blend well. Add pine nuts. Drop walnut-sized balls of dough into sugar and roll. Place on a greased cookie sheet.

Bake at 350 for 10 - 12 minutes or till golden.

Cookies & Considerations:

Tia, which is Portuguese for "aunt", reminded me to be grateful for the mountains we live in. She's still in awe, while I sometimes take them for granted - until they catch me by surprise, the way they sometimes do, sparkling in a peculiar light or caught at a glance, from an unusual angle!

Though living here is a choice, our heritage is a part of our journey that can't be changed. When I was in Grade 6, I was teased with nicknames. For a while, it was "Chiquita Banana". I don't know who, what, where, or how that originated, but later that year, I became "Porch Climber", after my Portuguese heritage.

These light, sponge-cake like cookies are in honor of my Portuguese heritage. Lemon is used often in baking, and pine nuts are native to Portugal. The Pine Trees bearing the cones that enclose these tiny, soft, white nuts, grow, in Portugal, like our Jack Pines grow here in the mountains - as if the one in charge knew exactly what to do and where to put them.

Chocolate Shortbread Cookies

2 cups flour
1/2 cup cocoa powder
1/2 tsp. salt
1 cup butter
3/4 cup icing sugar
1 tsp. vanilla

Combine flour, cocoa, and salt. Set aside. Beat butter till creamy. Add icing sugar and beat till light and fluffy. Add vanilla. Slowly add flour mixture and beat until well blended. Divide the dough into 4 pieces, roll each piece out, between wax paper, to an 5" circle, decorate the edge, much as you would a pie, and cut into 8 wedges. Place each wedge on a cookie sheet.
Bake at 325 for 10 - 15 minutes.

Cookies & Considerations:

A delectable chocolate shortbread - light, and if dipped in chocolate, decadent and rich, and very, very tasty.
Dough will puff and settle, crisping around the edges.
Melt some semi-sweet chocolate and drizzle or dunk one edge of the wedge!

"You have powers you never dreamed of. You can do things you never thought you cold do. There are no limitations in what you can do except the limitations of your own mind."
Darwin P. Kingsley

People on the Go

There's something therapeutic (and humbling) about kneeling in front of the toilet, brush in one hand, cleaner in the other, intent on the mundane task of tidying up the rubble and ruins of daily life.

We often put off housekeeping chores as long as we possibly can. While they are not necessarily a way of life for most of us, we usually prefer a clean and somewhat tidy home, to a home we feel the need to apologize for, when unexpected guests arrive.

I've given up apologizing about the kitchen counter.

On the day of housecleaning, and many times in between, we manage to free the counter of the undergrowth that continuously threatens it's subsistence. Still, it (miraculously) holds up 4 cars, a bear sitting on a ceramic chair and footstool, a helicopter, a castle, a couch and two kittens - all toys, a bird book, a magazine, a note pad, a permission slip, a remote (for the radio), a Lego® car, 2 page-a-day calendars, 3 juggling balls, a cordless phone, a power adapter for a CD player, a tensor bandage, 4 piles (divided) of assorted printed matter, 2 started bottles of wine (one red - blueberry actually, and one white), a calculator, and 2 watches, along with the usual (?) butter, jam (3 started jars), salt, pepper, sugar, cutting board, bread and napkins. There's another counter, but I suppose you get the picture. On a good day, it's chaos, clutter, confusion, and commotion. If (when) left unchecked - bedlam!

Some things you just have to accept. The fact is, no amount of complaining, wishing, planning, pleading, or simplifying is going to alter actuality. Unless we move out (again!), there's always going to be something on the counter, life is not tidy and orderly, and there's always something to do.

This is true whether we have nothing, more than we'll ever need, or somewhere in between. Whether it's daily, weekly, or monthly chores, cleaning toilets is just a hair's breadth layer off the glacier.

From three meals daily and the laundry, to watering plants and paying bills, to painting, repairing and replacing, the general upkeep of the home is like fighting a battle that can never be won.

Shall we call a truce then?

When we care for our homes, we are also making them more comfortable, content, warm, cozy, interesting, inviting, and humbling places for ourselves and those we love.

And since the house is clean, supper is ready to go, the laundry's put away, the plants are watered, the bills are paid and everyone is otherwise occupied for a moment, even though there's still more to do, lets just rest and be thankful, that we do have a toilet to clean and a home to mess up.

Food for thought:
How to ask for the bathroom in the language of the land:
'"Swedish - "Var fins det toaletten?"
Spanish - "Donde esta el bano?"
Russian - "Gd yeh tooahlyeht?"
Polish - "Gdzie jest lazienka?"
Japanese - "Toire wa doko desu ka?"
Italian - "Dove il gabinetto?"
Hungarian - "Hol van a fur doszoba?"
Greek - "Nerede tuvalet?"
German - "Wo ist die Toilette?"
French - "Ou est la toilette?"
Dutch - "Waar is het toilet?"
Danish - "Hvor er der toalette?"'
The Bathroom Guest Book

Rest!

Oatmeal Cookie Mix
Cookies & Considerations
on following page.

Oatmeal Cookie Mix

3 & 1/2 cups flour
3 & 1/2 cups rolled oats
1 & 3/4 cups sugar
1 cup brown sugar
4 tsp. baking powder
2 tsp. salt
2 cups shortening

Combine flour, oats, sugar, brown sugar, and salt. Cut in shortening. May be stored in a covered container, up to 6 weeks at room temperature, or freeze. Makes 12 cups.

To use:
3 cups Oatmeal Cookie Mix
1 egg
1 tsp. vanilla

Measure Oatmeal Cookie Mix by lightly spooning and leveling into a dry ingredient measuring cup. (Don't pack the mix.) Set aside. Beat egg and vanilla. Add cookie mix and stir till well combined. Add your own favorites or one of the following: 1/2 tsp. cinnamon, 1 cup of raisins and 1/2 cup of walnuts, or 1/3 cup each of milk, semisweet and butterscotch chips. Drop onto cookie sheets
Bake at 350 for 8 - 10 minutes or till golden.

Cookies & Considerations:
Even though it seems like they're getting shorter, there are still 24 hour in each day. Allocating time for things that need to get done is one way to stretch the day. Make even more time by stirring up a big batch of homemade Oatmeal Cookie Mix. You can store it and use it as you go to bake up yummy treats.

Hazelnut Crinkles

3 cup flour
2 tsp. baking powder
1/2 tsp. salt
1 cup chocolate-hazelnut spread
1/4 cup shortening
1 & 1/3 cups sugar
2 eggs
1 tsp. vanilla
1/3 cup milk
1/2 cup finely chopped, toasted hazelnuts
icing sugar

Combine flour, baking powder and salt. Set aside. Cream chocolate-hazelnut spread and shortening. Add sugar. Beat in eggs and vanilla. Add milk and flour mixture alternately. Add hazelnuts. Shape dough into balls and roll in powdered sugar.

Bake at 350 for 10 - 12 minutes or till surface is cracked and cookies are done.

Cookies & Considerations:

As we measure, mix, spoon and bake, we immerse ourselves in the construction of our undertaking. We see colors and feel textures. As the cookies bake, we smell the sweetness of the aromas and the blend of flavors. These cookies, with their sharp contrast of light and dark, are also a delight for the eyes. The end result is a palpable, tangible, wonderfully glorious, delectably delicious, edible work of art that is a delight for all the senses.

Shock Value - God is Not a Four-Letter Word!

"All the world's a stage and most of us are desperately unrehearsed."

That quote, by Sean O'Casey, may accurately describe how many of us feel when we hear about violence in the news, including the latest, based on religious hatred.

Does it shock us anymore? Or are we over anesthetized and medicated to the point that we've become so accustomed to the violence that, each time it happens, it takes more and more to shock us?

T. S. Elliot (1888 - 1965) envisioned that the approach of the millennium would have people shooting each other at random. We think it's not happening, it can't be so, but it is a widespread phenomenon. Statistics out of the United States show that over the past more than thirty years, crime has increased an astonishing 500%.

Consider the issues that affect us. Domestic violence, radical acts of terrorism, corruption, famine, destruction of the environment, ethnic wars of increasing intensity, hunger, poverty, disease, homelessness and hate crimes influence our lives. Every day, we are being reminded of violent crimes against humanity.

Why?

To bring us back home.

Somewhere along the way, a large part of the world strayed from belief in a higher power, religion and philosophy. Fear set in and walls were erected that would not tolerate differences. They were walls that even a powerful love could not pierce. Many of us gave up hope and began subsist on despair, anger, greed, prejudice, judgment, anxiety, jealousy and cowardice acts, born of fear. God became a frightening, four-letter word, so that even in many churches, the mention of God, or a higher power, became rare and discouraged.

But now? Now, we are being impelled to get back home. The movement we are undergoing is urging us get in touch with our own spiritual and religious convictions.

There are many spiritual and religious viewpoints. Over the years, religions have diverged and evolved to serve many needs and many cultures throughout the world. Now they are categorized according to the beliefs they share.

The twelve longest established and most prevalent religions in the world are Baha'i Faith, Confucianism, Shinto, Buddhism, Hinduism, Sikhism, Christianity, Islam, Jainism, Vootun, Taoism and Judaism, each with over 3 million followers. There are approximately 30 other ethical, spiritual, non-Christian and Neopagan religions and faiths. We are not here to criticize or attack any of them. There are no superior or inferior religions.

Somehow, they all speak the same language.

Call it religion. Call it spirituality. Whatever we call it, if we can realize that, ultimately, we all share the same God - a God who has allowed us such a richness of diversity, that we can each find our own way back home - then we can accept our differences and we can live in harmony.

At that point, we will find that it is no longer necessary to hold views based on fear. We can live our lives fulfilled, compassionate, loving, gracious, joyful and empowered. It's as simple as choosing to live a life based on the importance of conscious regard and consideration for our physical, mental, emotional and spiritual presence in the world.

Whether we practice one religion in particular, or spiritually embrace a combination of many, when we are able to tolerate and espouse the uniqueness of our world, spirituality and religion will work together for peace and devoted love.

Food for thought:
"No God, you say? Perhaps you're right;
I have no mystic, deep insight,
No knowledge of theology
To prove that God exists for me.
But, oh, the beauty of the hour
When winter's buds burst into flower
And fragrance fills the summertime breeze -
No God? Then who makes apple trees?"
Helen Lowrie Marshall

Espouse!

Apple Oatmeal
Cookies & Considerations
on following page.

Apple Oatmeal Cookies

2 cups flour
1 tsp. baking powder
1 tsp. baking soda
1 Tbsp. cinnamon
1 tsp. salt
1 cup butter
3/4 cup brown sugar
3/4 cup sugar
4 eggs
2 tsp. vanilla
4 cup rolled oats
1 cup diced apples
1 cup chopped walnuts

Optional:
1 cup icing sugar
1/4 cup whipping cream

Combine flour, baking powder, baking soda, cinnamon and salt. Cream butter and sugars. Beat in eggs and vanilla. Gradually blend in flour mixture. Add oats, apples and walnuts. Drop onto baking sheets.

Bake at 350 for 12 - 15 minutes or till golden. If desired, combine icing sugar and whipping cream and drizzle over cooled cookies.

Cookies & Considerations:

I thank God for apple trees and the apples to make this soft, moist, cake-like cookie. With apple season just beginning, it's a beautiful way to appreciate the mystic wonders all around us, including what it takes to make an apple.

Chocolate Chunk Peanut Butter Cookies

2 & 1/2 cups flour
1 tsp. baking soda
1 tsp. baking powder
1 tsp. salt
1 cup butter or margarine
1 cup peanut butter
1 cup sugar
1 cup brown sugar
2 eggs
1 - 300 gram pkg. chocolate chunks or chips

Combine flour, baking soda, baking powder and salt. Set aside. Cream butter, peanut butter, sugars and eggs. Blend in flour mixture. Add chocolate. Drop onto cookie sheet and press with fork, making a criss-cross.
Bake at 350 for 10 - 12 minutes.

Cookies & Considerations:

If being a cool mom was suddenly defined by my abilities to play video games, I wouldn't be very cool. I can't play but when I try to, I laugh till I cry, and thank heaven when I get a "time out" so that I can gain a modicum of control over myself. I just can't get my fingers to make the buttons do what my brain wants them to.

If I move at all - something I believe to be somewhat important in a racing game - it's usually in circles against the walls. When I did get going, one of my sons told me I was funny. He also mentioned that I was going the wrong way. (I knew that!)

Need I say, I have yet to finish a lap in anything other than last place. But I have fun doing it and thankfully, my children don't measure my success at motherhood by how well I play video games. This is one of their favorite cookies.

Swatting Contest

I have a confession to make. For the last three weeks or so, I've been feeding the wildlife.

I haven't been the only one though! I've seen signs that others have also been feeding the wildlife. Not on purpose, sure. And if we could help it, not at all.

You can tell who we are. We're the ones doing the Swat 'n Itch Boogie. The bumping, jarring and shimmying gyrations are a sure indication that we have become targets of the ubiquitous mosquito.

It isn't so much that we've been feeding them, as they've been feeding on us. With 2000 - 3000 species of mosquitoes throughout the world, there is one variety or another to be found almost everywhere, from the tropics to the Arctic Circle, from sea level to mountaintop.

And, almost everywhere, it is the female of the species who uses a hypodermic-like mouthpiece to pierce our skin and suck our blood. They inject salivary fluid into the stab to prevent our blood from clotting, which also blesses us with swelling, itching and sometimes infectious diseases.

In some native cultures, each prick from this unladylike insect is also believed to bless us with the gift of distraction. What a stroke of good fortune!

With a Friday the 13th coming up, as illogical or unreasonable as it may seem, many beliefs and superstitions will be observed. Having been derived from a multitude of influences, some superstitions may include the use of salt, the right foot, four-leaf clovers, white elephants, remembrances and traditions, potions, ladders, knocking on wood or trees, the moon, the stars, mirrors, umbrellas, colors, buildings, numbers, horseshoes and rabbit's feet, as well as animals.

While it may seem illogical or unreasonable to some, for others, it is believed that each animal we encounter, whether physically, spiritually or through our dreams, is sent to help us. It is thought that we may call upon animals to provide us with whatever instinctive qualities we need in order to see solutions to overcoming our challenges.

There is a popular quote by Reinhold Neibuhr. It goes, "God, grant me the serenity to accept the things I cannot change, the courage to change the things I can, and the wisdom to know the difference."

When mosquitoes target us as the source of their next feast, we may start swatting at them, allowing them to show us how stresses, distractions and imbalance can cause us to react blindly. Or, we can use mosquitoes to help us increase our focus and determination by honoring and accepting them and the awareness they offer us.

Acceptance is not resignation or submission, nor denial. Acceptance is acknowledging that we have no choice over situations, people and things that are not the way we want them to be. In a situation where we are at odds, acceptance is the only choice we always have.

So, if a mosquito targets us for a free meal, we are not at liberty to choose distraction and imbalance. Perhaps we can enthusiastically accept the reality that we share the planet with them and give thanks for focus, determination and the ability to react with acceptance.

Food for thought:
"Almost any event will put on a new face when received with cheerful acceptance."
Henry S. Haskins

Focus!

Date Pinwheels
Cookies & Considerations
on following page.

Date Pinwheel Cookies

Filling:
1 & 1/2 cups chopped dates
1/2 cup sugar
2/3 cup water
1/4 cup finely chopped pecans

Dough:
3 & 1/4 cups flour
1 Tbsp. baking powder
1/2 tsp. salt
1 cup butter
2 cups brown sugar
1 tsp. vanilla
2 eggs

Filling:
In a small pan, combine dates, sugar and water. Bring to a boil. Reduce heat and simmer 5 minutes. Stir in pecans and allow mixture to cool.

Dough:
Combine flour, baking powder and salt. Set aside. Cream butter and brown sugar. Add vanilla. Add eggs, one at a time. Add flour mixture and mix well. Cover dough or wrap in plastic and chill for 1 hour.

On a floured surface, roll dough into a 10" x 10" square. Carefully spread with date mixture. (Warm it in the microwave for 30 seconds, if necessary.) On one edge, start rolling dough (like a jellyroll). Wrap and chill for 2 hours.

Slice into 1/4" slices. Place on a greased cookie sheet and bake at 350 for 10 - 12 minutes, or till golden.

Cookies & Considerations:

These classic cookies, shaped like targets, might not give the mosquitoes something else to focus on, but making them might be enough of a distraction that you'll be able to cheerfully accept them.

Chocolate Chunk Oatmeal Cookies

4 cups flour
4 & 1/2 cups rolled oats
1 tsp. baking powder
2 tsp. baking soda
2 tsp. salt
2 cups butter
2 cups sugar
2 cups brown sugar
4 eggs
2 tsp. vanilla
12 oz. bag semi-sweet chocolate chips, chunks or grated chocolate

Combine flour, oats, baking powder, baking soda and salt. Set aside. Cream butter. Add sugars. Add eggs and vanilla. Mix in chocolate chunks. Drop onto cookie sheets.
Bake at 350 for 12 - 15 minutes.

Cookies & Considerations:
The recipe for success is to be humble, tolerant and kind. The recipe for failure is to try to impress everybody else but you. One is difficult to achieve. The other is difficult to endure.
We each have our successes. Here's an easy, nutritious and yummy way to achieve success in baking.

Spiritual Intention

Last night, as I drifted off to sleep, I uttered a prayer of intention.

It was my intention to wake up in the morning with a topic or a clear idea for my next column. As Stephen Crotts says, though, "God has editing rights over our prayers. He will edit them, correct them, bring them in line with His will and then hand them back to us to be resubmitted."

The answer to my prayer of intention came when I realized that "intention" was the topic I'd been presented to write about.

"Intent" is the birthplace of "cause and effect" and the homestead of "the thought that counts".

To a large degree, the dimension of spirituality in our daily lives is comprised of our intentions. Conversely, our intentions reflect the dimensions of our days.

What we intend for others, becomes the basis of our own spiritual existence.

When our intentions are to project love, show compassion and demonstrate a greater understanding, we grow spiritually.

Not all intentions are based on spiritual development though. When no thought is given to the soul or spirituality, our conduct often revolves around behaviors which intend hurt and harm, and which demonstrate anger, cynicism, greed, vengeance, prejudice and jealousy. When we strive to create destruction, we strive to destroy ourselves.

Our conscious and unconscious energy comes back to us. Even when things don't turn out well, if we have intended to do them for the greater good, and if we've done them with the best intentions, our subconscious motivation is what shapes our experiences. Knowing in our hearts that we've never intended or calculated to maliciously harm anyone is to live with spiritual intent.

The truth behind our actions, thoughts and behaviors, what we feel, what we think, how we behave, how we live, what we value, what we plan for or aim at, what we propose to do, is the basis of our deeds or misdeeds.

We are living a sound and spiritual life if we can measure our own conduct through harmless, pure design and in the name of truly helping others. Our best spiritual intentions are never wasted. Doing good is doing well.

When we see a beggar on the street, it's easy to criticize, judge and question. But if we desire to live our lives with the intent is to show compassion, we should check what's inside.

If our hearts are understanding, then it is right to offer money.

If, however, we feel guilt for going by without giving, if we pass judgment on someone else's circumstances which we do not know enough about, or if we are cynical, doubtful and suspicious, then it isn't coming from our heart. Whatever we give, will not have been born of love and spiritual intention.

Food for thought:
"What you intend is what you become. If you intend to take as much from life and others as you can, if your thoughts are of taking instead of giving, you create a reality that reflects your intentions . . .you create a taking reality."
Gary Zukav

Intend!

Caramel Pecan Shortbread Tart
Cookies & Considerations
on following page.

Caramel Pecan Shortbread Tart

Shortbread Crust:
1 & 1/2 cup flour
1/2 tsp. salt
1/2 cup butter
2 Tbsp. sugar
1 egg
1/4 tsp. vanilla
Caramel Pecan Filling:
1/2 cup butter
2 Tbsp. honey
2 Tbsp. sugar
1/2 cup brown sugar
1 cup pecans
2 Tbsp. whipping cream
Chocolate Topping:
1/3 cup whipping cream
2/3 cup semisweet chocolate chips

Shortbread Crust:
>   Combine flour and salt. Set aside. Cream together butter and sugar until light and fluffy. Add flour mixture and combine until mixture resembles course crumbs. Add egg and vanilla and mix until combined and dough comes together. Press into or roll out to fit bottom and sides of an 8" or 9" cake pan. Set aside.

Caramel Pecan Filling:
>   In a small pan, melt together butter, honey, sugar and brown sugar. Cook over medium heat until mixture comes to a boil. Boil for 3 minutes. Remove from heat and stir in pecans and cream. Pour over prepared crust and bake at 350 for 30 minutes. Cool completely and remove from pan.

Chocolate Topping:
>   In a small pan, heat cream almost to boiling. Remove from heat and stir in chocolate. Whisk until smooth and pour topping over tart. Allow to set. Cut into wedges and serve.

Cookies & Considerations:
>   This large, layered cookie, which is baked in a cake pan, is intended to be sliced and served in wedges. With a buttery shortbread crust, a gooey caramel pecan filling and a luscious chocolate topping, it is also intended to be smooth and crumbly, gooey and crunchy, delightfully delectable, and absolutely decadent.

Linzer Cookies

1 cup sliced almonds
2 cups flour, divided
2 Tbsp. cocoa
1 tsp. cinnamon
1/4 tsp. cloves
1/4 tsp. salt
1 cup butter
3/4 cup icing sugar
2 egg yolks
1 tsp. grated lemon zest
raspberry jam
icing sugar

Combine almonds and 1/2 cup of flour in food processor. Process till almonds are finely ground. Add remaining flour, cocoa, cinnamon, cloves and salt. Process once more just to blend. Set aside. Cream butter and sugar till light. Add egg yolks and lemon zest. Beat in flour mixture till well combined. Divide dough into 4 and wrap in plastic. Refrigerate for 1 - 2 hours or till firm. On a flour surface, roll out dough to 1/8" thick. Cut with cookie cutter. Cut out a hole in half of the cookies.

Place on baking sheets and bake at 350 for 10 - 12 minutes. Cool. Spread bottom of hole-less cookies with jam (about 1 tsp.). Heavily sprinkle icing sugar over the other cookies (the ones with holes) and place on top of jam.

Cookies & Considerations:

The only thing better than one cookie is two. These traditional sandwich cookies could become the treasured treats that your family asks for by special request. Make them for those you love and they're sure to be a hit.

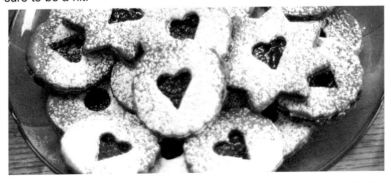

Some Things Kids Need Every Day -
And Some Things They Need A Lot More

Our children are back to school following spring break. Hopefully the holidays were enjoyable and some basic needs were met.

To initiate their arrival for the final stretch of the school year, I've prepared a quiz for our children. It is about some things they need every day and some things they need a lot more.

Since the questions have no correct answers, grading them will be a snap. The answers may become an open invitation to discover, cultivate and enlarge our relationships with our children.

The rules for the children are: no studying, no copying and answer all questions with the best intentions.

For the parents, the requirements are simple: eyes that are open to see, ears that are open to hear, an open mind that's full of curiosity and an open heart that is full of love and courage.

Ask your children to respond to these questions on a piece of paper.
WARNING: this quiz in not for the faint of heart or of spirit!

#1.) What is the one thing you want to do and your parents won't let you?

#2.) What one thing were you first afraid to tell, but after you did, you were glad?

#3.) When you think of your Mom, what do you think?

#4.) When you think of your Dad, what do you think?

#5.) Do you think your parents are ever afraid? If yes, what do you think your parents are afraid of?

#6.) What do you like best?

#7.) What do you like least?

#8.) Should you have as many things as you want?

#9.) What is your favorite memory?

#10.) In the whole world, what bothers you most?

#11.) Do you think it's tougher on you being a kid now, than it was on your parents? If yes, in what way?

#12.) What do you like doing with your parents that takes 1 minute?

#13.) My proudest moment was:

#14.) Would you like to do something silly and fun with your parents?

If so, what would it be?

      #15.) What do you really want your parents to teach you?

      #16.) Do you know that your parents love you?

      (If you can't ask your children these questions face to face, cut this out and mail it to them along with a piece of paper and a self addressed, stamped envelope.)

Food for thought:

"We, the children, need the following:

We need encouragement, we need to laugh, we need inspiration.

We need to be read to.

We need to have self esteem, love & security, adventure, discipline & freedom.

We need to make mistakes, ask questions, to imagine.

We need to learn and sometimes, we need to lose.

We need to be hugged.

We need family, friends & even foes.

And heroes.

We need nourishment."

From my favorite commercial for Kellogg's® cereal.

Need!

Cereal
Cookies & Considerations
on following page.

Cereal Cookies

1 & 3/4 cups flour
1 & 3/4 cups whole wheat flour
1 tsp. salt
2 tsp. baking soda
3 cups rolled oats
1 cup coconut
1 & 1/3 cups wheat germ
2 cups butter
2 & 1/2 cups brown sugar
1 Tbsp. vanilla
4 eggs
1 cup raisins
1 cup milk chocolate chips
4 cups flake-type cereal

Combine flour, whole wheat flour, salt, baking soda, rolled oats, coconut and wheat germ. Set aside. Cream butter and brown sugar until light and fluffy. Add vanilla and eggs. Blend well. Add flour mixture and mix well. Stir in flake-type cereal, raisins and chocolate chips. Drop onto greased cookie sheets and flatten slightly.

Bake at 350 for 8 - 10 minutes, or till golden brown.

Cookies & Considerations:

Some things, kids need every day. Some things, they need a lot more.

Our children need us to let them talk, while we listen to them very carefully. They need us to consider their words important. They need us to be present with our time. They need us to make them priorities. Our children need us to show warmth. And most importantly, our children want, and need, our unconditional love.

Our children need nourishment and here's a warm and loving way to show it, with a big batch of fiber rich, nutrition packed, chewy cookies.

Cashew Butter Cookies

3 cups flour
1 tsp. baking soda
1/2 tsp. salt
2 cups cashews
1/2 cup honey
2 Tbsp. milk
1 tsp. vanilla
1 cup butter
1 cup brown sugar
Finely chopped cashews for rolling

Combine flour, baking soda, and salt. Set aside. In a food processor, grind cashews. Add honey, milk, and vanilla. Process until mixture resembles coarsely ground peanut butter. Set aside. Cream butter. Add brown sugar. Add processed cashew mixture and blend well. Add flour mixture. Shape into balls and roll in remaining cashews. Flatten cookie slightly with the bottom of a glass dipped in sugar.

Bake at 350 for 10 - 12 minutes.

Cookies & Considerations:

These cookies contain a fair share of surprises, much like our futures. A cashew butter - made with ground cashews, vanilla, and milk (recipe included) - is the base for this delightful, shortbread-like cookie.

The Evolution and Resolutions of New Year's Eve

The earliest known recordings of a New Year's festival date back to 2000 BC. With celebrations taking place from early spring in mid-March, to the autumn equinox in September, and the winter solstice in December, the dates for the festivities has been evolving, as we have been resolving.

In Japan, New Year's festivities take place on January 1st to 3rd, except in the rural areas which sometimes celebrate the New Year closer to the time of the Chinese New Year, between January 20 and February 19. In South India, the Tamil New Year still takes place during the winter solstice. The Jewish New Year, Rosh Hashanah, starts on the first day of the month Tishri, which may begin between September 6th to October 5th on the Gregorian calendar.

In 1582, the Roman Catholic church reinstated January 1st as the date for New Year's Day for all who use the Gregorian calendar. During the following 350 years, other countries adopted the same date to celebrate the New Year. Russia, in 1918, was the last major nation to follow in agreement.

As part of the celebration, to honor the start of a New Year, many of us make a New Year's resolution. It is a resolve we make to ourselves with hopes of somehow improving the quality of our lives. In our proclamation, we often declare a desire to break a habit which we believe is harmful to ourselves.

Sometimes our resolve is for something we desire to do (lose weight, quit smoking, get more exercise, cut back on caffeine, cut out junk food, eat properly, spend more time with our loved ones). Sometimes our resolve is for something we'd like not to do (drugs, alcohol, lie, steal, crack our knuckles, bite our nails, belch, procrastinate, be late, forget, or clean obsessively).

The element that bad habits have in common is that everyone has them. Some habits become as natural to us as the next breath we take. Although there are ways to break bad habits, they often involve time, patience, and perseverance. With spunk, tenacity, desire, commitment and a strong resolve, we may help turn harmful, patterns into positive, healthy, endeavors.

However, if you've already broken your New Year's resolution, you are in the company of seventy-seven percent of us, who will break our New

Year's resolutions, within the first week of the New Year! If you've already broken your resolution, and are looking for a new one, think about this.

Many of us are harshest on ourselves. We are willing to nit pick at our imperfections, when no one else would. And even when there are already others doing the job for us, we're still willing to tear ourselves to shreds over our faults and shortcomings.

Acceptably, none of us is without faults, but what if we resolve to treat ourselves with greater kindness anyway? What if we formally express our declaration to be easier on ourselves? What if we lay down our armor and proclaim that there is not anyone we should be so critical, judgmental and unforgiving of - especially not ourselves? What if we decree that no soul should be treated so harshly or with such impatience?

Let us resolve to have greater acceptance of ourselves. Let us be calm and at peace, comfortable and content. Let us be natural and unburdened.

As certain as the New Year has just begun, let us be certain that we have just begun. Let us resolve to greet the New Year with the clarity of belief in our own power and brightness and with acceptance of our imperfections and our perfections.

Food for thought:
"To accept ourselves as we are means to value our imperfections as much as our perfections."
Sandra Bierig

Resolve!

Applesauce Date Spice
Cookies & Considerations
on following page.

Applesauce Date Spice Cookies

2 cups flour
1 tsp. baking soda
1 tsp. baking powder
1 tsp. salt
1 tsp. allspice
1 tsp. ginger
1 tsp. cloves
2 tsp. cinnamon
3 cups rolled oats
1 & 1/2 cups applesauce
1 cup brown sugar
1/2 cup corn syrup
2 egg whites
2 tsp. vanilla
1 cup finely chopped dates

Combine flour, baking soda, baking powder, salt, allspice, ginger, cloves, cinnamon and rolled oats. Set aside. In a large bowl, combine the applesauce, brown sugar, corn syrup, egg whites and vanilla. Add flour mixture. Stir in dates. Drop onto un-greased baking sheet. With wet palms, flatten each cookie.

Bake 12 minutes or until edges turn golden.

Cookies & Considerations:

Let us celebrate the New Year with the acceptance of this soft, chewy, cookie that's full of fiber and free of fat. (It shouldn't break many resolves.) Whatever our imperfections and perfections, may we have a Happy New Year!

Rugelach

2 cups flour
1 cup butter
1 cup vanilla ice cream
approx. 1 cup strawberry jam
approx. 5 oz. semi-sweet chocolate, chopped fine
approx. 1 cup pecans, chopped fine
icing sugar

Beat butter & flour. Add ice cream and beat till dough holds together. Divide dough in half. Roll each half out to a 9 x 16 rectangle. Spread with jam. Sprinkle with chocolate and nuts. Roll up lengthwise (like a wrap) and tuck in ends. Place on greased or parchment lined cookie sheet. Cut diagonal slits in roll.

Bake at 350 for 20 - 25 minutes or till golden. Cool, sprinkle with icing sugar and slice.

Cookies & Considerations:

The smell of freshly baked cookies is one of the most heavenly scents. These cookies aren't traditional or classic, but they are a recipe I have previously, zealously guarded.

I've seen and tried variations of this recipe, usually containing cream cheese. The ice cream is a stretch (not a standard ingredient, for sure). It might seem "out there", but try it. You'll love the fabulous flavors, and the myriad of textures, as well as the intrigue involved in creating tasty treasures. Roll them up like a "wrap", bake them whole, then slice them like a biscotti and indulge.

I promise you won't regret including it in your new list of favorites.

The Gift of Giving

In Dr. Seuss's "How the Grinch Stole Christmas", the Grinch thinks he can stop Christmas from coming by removing objects.

The Grinch makes the 10,000 foot trek up Mt. Crumpet, with a sleigh fully laden with the Christmas cargo he stole, only to realize that Christmas doesn't come from a store - "it means just a little bit more". Even with "no ribbons, no tags, no packages, boxes or bags", Christmas comes to the Who's down in Whoville.

Like the Grinch, we have come to associate gift-giving with Christmas. So much so, that the true meaning of the holiday is sometimes overshadowed.

There's no disputing it - Christmas gift-giving is big business! Like the Grinch, we often assign meaning to objects. Through the Great Depression, it was yo-yos, BB guns and other cowboy and cops-and-robbers paraphernalia. Also big, were war toys and toy soldiers.

The 50's brought the persistently popular "Etch-A-Sketch", "Silly Putty", "Frisbees", "Hula Hoops", "Mr. Potato Head", "Lego", "The Game of Life", "Pogo Sticks", "Matchbox Cars", "Play Doh", electric trains, "Barbie", the Davy Crockett coonskin hat, as well as the television set.

During the 60's, "G. I. Joe", Beatles records, "Tonka Trucks", the "Slinky", "The Mousetrap Game", "Yahtzee", "Scrabble", "Operation!", "Twister" and color T. V. were all the rage.

The 70's brought the novelty "I Am Not a Crook" watches, beaming with the image of President Nixon, whose eyes shifted back and forth with the ticking of each second! Eight tracks, were popular, as were CB radios, troll dolls with tufts of intensely glowing, iridescent hair and "Spirograph". Reaching new heights of commercial prosperity was anything to do with George Lucas' "Star Wars", as well as pet rocks and mood rings.

The 80's focused on "Cabbage Patch" dolls, "Smurfs", exercise bikes, ice cream makers, "Trivial Pursuit", and consumer electronics, such as CD players, video cameras, laptops and "Nintendo".

The "Teenage Mutant Ninja Turtles" led us into the 90's, along with "Bart Simpson" and the "Power Rangers", but virtual pets, "Elmo", "Furby", and "Pokemon" will take us into the next millennium along with a few of the toys we used to play with as children.

In addition, the years have been rich with other gifts - the gifts we give of ourselves. And like the Grinch, who's heart grew three sizes that day, when we give of ourselves, our open hearts grow.

The gift of listening, when we ask someone how they are, is the gift of compassion, kindness and caring. The gift of helping a disabled or elderly person by being a companion, taking them shopping or out for a walk or dinner, to appointments or errands, is the gift of freedom, acceptance and understanding. The gift of volunteering is a way to reach out to help others. It is the gift of discovery, nurturing and generosity. The gift of forgiveness is the gift of trust, faith and second chances. The gift of time is the gift of selflessness, wonder and love.

In giving of ourselves, we give others the gift of courage, the inspiration to get involved and to give of themselves. The gifts we give ourselves are appreciation, and abundance.

We also give ourselves the treasure of the true essence of Christmas - global goodwill, one world united, giving back to the community, practicing random acts of kindness, doing the right thing, people helping people, sharing love and giving love.

Gift-giving should come from the heart. Gifts that have meaning are given with love and are priceless, regardless of how much they cost. Our holiday decrees should not be what to buy and for whom, but what do we believe in and how do we instill the shining brightness of those beliefs in others.

Yes, Christmas is about gifts, and the best ones are difficult to wrap, harder to give and don't fit under the tree.

Food for Thought:
"Welcome Christmas, as we stand, heart-to-heart and hand-to-hand."
The Who's of Whoville, Dr. Seuss's How the Grinch Stole Christmas

Give!

Raisin
Cookies & Considerations
on following page.

Raisin Cookies

4 cups flour
2 tsp. baking powder
1 tsp. salt
2 tsp. cinnamon
1 tsp. nutmeg
1 tsp. allspice
1 tsp. cloves
1 cup butter
1 cup sugar
1 cup brown sugar
4 eggs
1/2 cup milk
2 tsp. vanilla
2 cups raisins
1 1/2 cups walnuts

Combine flour, baking powder, salt, cinnamon, nutmeg, allspice, and cloves. Set aside. Cream butter and sugars. Add eggs, milk and vanilla. Stir in dry ingredients. Add raisins and walnuts. Blend well. Drop onto cookie sheets. Flatten slightly.

Bake at 350 for 10 - 12 minutes.

Cookies & Considerations:

A gift for Helen. She needed a recipe for her husband, who likes a soft, spicy, raisin cookie with no "porridge". These cookies give the gift of half the fat and sugar. To help her (and you) welcome Christmas. . .

Chocolate Hazelnut Hearts

3/4 cup (5 oz) semisweet chocolate, melted
1 & 1/4 cups flour
3/4 cup icing sugar
2/3 cup hazelnuts, toasted and ground
1/4 tsp. instant espresso coffee powder
1/4 tsp. salt
1/2 cup butter
2 tsp. vanilla
4 oz. semisweet chocolate
white chocolate for drizzling

Melt chocolate and set aside to cool. Combine flour, sugar, hazelnuts, coffee powder and salt. Set aside. Beat butter. Add melted chocolate and vanilla. Add flour mixture and beat till dough comes together. Roll out dough on floured surface. Cut with heart shaped cookie cutter.

Bake 8 to 10 minutes. Cool.

Melt semisweet chocolate and dip parts of hearts. Drizzle with melted white chocolate.

Cookies & Considerations:

These nutty hearts have a hint of coffee and a suggestion of chocolate. Slightly decadent, but then your Sweetheart is worth it! Have a really Happy Valentine's Day, Love!

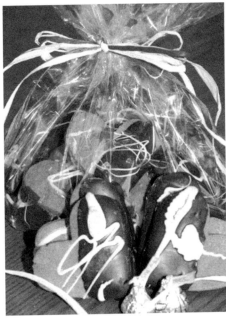

Understanding Unique and Distinct

Today, I watched a man and woman each walk their dogs across the street.

The man, with a black and white Spaniel, was first. The Spaniel was highly, uh, enthusiastic!? It walked in circles as it crossed, bouncing, leaping, lively, tongue wagging, ears flapping, every fiber energized. It simply could not, and would not contain it's exuberance. And that, I suppose, is as it should be.

Behind that pair, came the lady with a Beagle.

The Beagle pranced delicately. It's paws barely touched the ground, as they were delicately placed upon the pavement. Not a hair out of place, the beagle appeared to float as it strolled across the street, head high and proud, nose to the sky, posture exquisitely majestic, stately and poised. And that, I suppose, is also as it should be.

Apparently, by the look of disdain (or was it embarrassment) on the Beagle's face, the Beagle would rather not have to cross the street at the same time as the seemingly uncouth Spaniel. While the Beagle looked down it's nose, the Spaniel happily carried on. Springing forth, the excitable Spaniel was oblivious that the haughty Beagle would rather that the ardent Spaniel take itself around the corner and get a hold of itself.

If opposites attract, these two should definitely get together!

Understanding our differences is an effective tool. We nourish each other by understanding one another. We encourage others to understand us, by first understanding them. The rest falls naturally into place allowing us to nourish ourselves as well.

Mastering the art of understanding unusual behavior, idiosyncrasies and peculiarities affords us the ability to see with compassion. When we are able to see things from another perspective we stop taking them personally and, not only tolerate, but honor differences. The potential for conflict can be dramatically reduced when we allow ourselves to see others with compassion and understanding, instead of aggravation and annoyance.

The challenge is to see spiritual beauty in the unique differences, and to find them all equally as beautiful - no matter how unique. When we learn to do this, we will have learnt to nurture the soul. Magical things will happen. Everyday things will enchant. Peaceful feelings will emerge. Aspects of daily life that we may not previously have noticed will suddenly contain a touch of grace. We will remember what makes ordinary things special.

The fact is, that you and I may see different things in distinctly different ways. If one of us is not seeing the beauty, it does not mean that the beauty does not exist. Rather, it might suggest that one of us is not looking carefully enough, or with the right perspective.

Consider the fact that our principle differences are vast. Expect them to be. Then, respectfully appreciate your own uniqueness and allow yourself to feel love and appreciation for the uniqueness of others.

Food for thought:
"Variety's the very spice, that gives it all it's flavor."
William Cowper

Appreciate!

Krumiri
Cookies & Considerations
on following page.

Krumiri

1 & 1/2 cups flour
1 cup white or yellow cornmeal
1/4 tsp. salt
1 cup butter
2/3 cup white sugar
1 tsp. vanilla
3 egg yolks

Combine flour, cornmeal and salt. Set aside. Cream butter with sugar and vanilla till fluffy. Add egg yolks, one at a time. Stir in flour mixture. Add currants. Form dough into balls. Place on greased baking sheet. Press flat with the bottom of a glass dipped in sugar.

Bake at 325 for 15 - 17 minutes or till light brown around edges.

Cookies & Considerations:

These cookies are unique and distinct. With cornmeal and currants, I enjoy the unusual blend of a variety of flavors and textures. They have soul, essence and spirit. I hope you do too.

Pecan Shortbread

3 & 1/2 cups flour
1/2 tsp. salt
2 cups butter
1 cup sugar
1 tsp. vanilla
2 cups toasted pecans

Measure flour and salt. Set aside. Cream butter and sugar. Add vanilla. Add flour gradually. Add pecans. Form dough into balls, roll in sugar and flatten with the bottom of a glass.
Bake at 325 for 12 to 15 minutes.

Cookies & Considerations:
On the risk of changing . . . no courage needed for these simple crispy, nutty shortbread. Take a risk if you dare, and change them by dipping them in chocolate.

"It takes courage to push yourself to places that you have never been before . . . to test your limits . . . to break through barriers."
Source Unknown

Top O' the Mornin' to Ya!

He is one of history 's most successful missionaries.

Saint Patrick was born in Britain in 385A.D. At age 16, Patrick was kidnapped by Irish pirates. He worked as a shepherd, in Ireland, for six years before escaping to Gaul (now France). He became a priest, then a bishop and eventually returned to Ireland to teach his gospel to the same people who had once kidnapped and enslaved him.

Patrick spent nearly thirty years introducing Christianity to Ireland. It was one of his greatest accomplishments and for that, he has remained their hero and the patron saint of Ireland.

In his honor, Ireland celebrates with a five day festival. This country-wide holiday is rich with charm, pomp and pageantry. It is integrated with parades, music, magicians, clowns, stilt walkers, fireworks, street performances and dances.

Over here, we celebrate St. Patrick's Day with not quite as much grandeur. We tint our food and beverages green and eat things like Irish Stew and Irish Soda Bread. We wear "Kiss me, I'm Irish" pins and green clothes. We also think about how we can bring ourselves a little of the "luck o' the Irish" that also commemorates St. Patrick's Day.

The Irish symbolize good fortune with horseshoes, rainbows, pots of gold, four leaf clovers and leprechauns.

The world over, many people believe that pink pigs, green frogs, elephants with their trunks raised, chimes, bells and rabbit's feet are lucky charms. (I don't know if the rabbit would agree.)

In Britain and Australia, black cats are actually considered good luck, especially if one crosses your path. Simply greeting the cat politely releases good fortune.

Mike Wallace says "Motivation triggers luck." A Yiddish proverb says, 'Better an ounce of luck than a pound of gold.' Oprah Winfrey says, "Luck is a matter of preparation meeting opportunity." Tennesse Williams said, "Luck is believing you're lucky."

Acceptably, there are many views on what "luck" actually is.

Some believe that luck is created through hard work and built step by step. Based on the principle of cause and effect, through logical and level-headed thinking, with good timing, boldness, courage, experience, persistence and common sense, we maximize our luck.

Others believe that an upbeat attitude and a dazzling nature is the best source of luck. Chance encounters are considered lucky breaks. Accidents are "meant to be". "Lady luck", "fate", "old man destiny" and "written in the stars", are given credit for unexpected gains.

Yet others believe in a combination of any or all of the above, hoping for, but not counting on luck.

As for the phrase, "the luck o' the Irish". . . it is said that Saint Patrick's own personality was "unusually winning"!

Food for thought:
"If a man who cannot count finds a four-leaf clover, is he lucky?"
Stanislaw J. Lec

Charm!

> *Irish Flag or Lucky Shamrock*
> Cookies & Considerations
> *on following page.*

Irish Flag or Lucky Shamrock Cookies

2 & 1/2 cups flour
1 tsp. baking soda
1 tsp. cream of tartar
1/2 tsp. salt
1 cup butter
1 & 1/2 cups icing sugar
1 tsp. vanilla
1 egg

Icing:
1 cup icing sugar
1/2 tsp. vanilla
1/4 cup whipping cream
2 drops orange food coloring
2 drops green food coloring

Combine flour, baking soda, cream of tartar and salt. Set aside. Cream butter and add icing sugar. Beat in vanilla and egg. Mix well. Blend in flour mixture. Roll dough out to 1/4" thickness. For flag cookies, cut out rectangles 2" x 3", or use shamrocks and other cookie cutters.

Bake at 350 for 8 - 10 minutes or until lightly browned. Cool, frost and let set.

For icing, combine all ingredients, whisking in enough cream to make the frosting spreadable. For flags, divide frosting into 2 small bowls, adding orange coloring to one bowl and green to the other. Make a 1" wide green stripe on the left side of the cookie rectangles, and a 1" orange stripe on the right side, leaving the middle inch, unfrosted.

Cookies & Considerations:

Lucky for me - whether it was written in the stars or good timing - in the spirit of officially celebrating St. Patrick's Day, an "unusually winning" lady printed the basis for this recipe, for a crisp St. Patrick's Day sugar cookie, off the Internet for me.

Tomorrow (March 17th) is St. Patrick's Day, but if you're reading this on Saturday or Sunday, you're in luck!

As fate would have it, you can use the same recipe, cut the cookies out with flower shapes and tint the icing pink and yellow to honor the arrival of the first official day of spring, March 21st. How fortunate.

Three Hole Cookies
(Drei Augen)

4 & 2/3 cups flour
1 cup almonds, toasted and finely ground
2 tsp. cinnamon
2 & 1/2 cups butter
1 & 1/3 cup sugar
icing sugar for dusting
1 cup red currant jelly

Combine flour, ground almonds and cinnamon. Set aside. Cream butter and sugar until light and fluffy. Add flour mixture. On a lightly floured surface, roll out dough. Cut with a 1 & 1/2 inch round cookie cutter. With a large straw, cut out 3 small holes in half of the cookies.

Bake at 350 for 12 minutes, or till lightly browned. Cool.

Boil jelly for 2 minutes and cool slightly. Dust the cutout cookies with icing sugar. Turn over the solid cookies, so that bottom side is up. Spoon or brush each bottom with jelly and top with a cutout cookie. Press lightly so jam fills the holes.

Cookies & Considerations:

Drei Augen means "three eyes" in German. The eyes are the three small holes atop these cookies. Their blend of flavorful almonds and spicy cinnamon, tangy jam and sweet icing sugar is a contrast and combination sure to make this truly a cookie people everywhere would love.

You're Doing Fine - Just Keep Pedaling

I was the last one in our family to learn how to ride a bike. Like some people who never feel the need to learn how to drive a car, I hadn't felt the urge to progress from my tricycle to a two-wheeler.

Until . . . I hit a rock going full steam ahead and flipped myself head over handlebars. I landed on a rock with my chin, where a scar still reminds me of my traumatic childhood experience.

That's when I started riding the smallest two-wheeler ever known to humankind, after which I progressed to the biggest two-wheeler ever known to humankind (the in between size was always taken!).

It's been a long time since I've encouraged even my own kids to learn to ride a bicycle, but the words "you're doing fine - just keep pedaling" are applicable in many other ways.

How many times, in many different situations, do those very words, or words that imply the same sense of encouragement, help us to reach higher and search deeper for the courage to continue?

I used them just today, in a silent prayer of encouragement to a young elk.

In the early morning dawn, a herd of elk crossed the road, came into our back yard, continued across an open field and jumped over a fence. Of the 13 or so males, females and young ones, all managed to jump the fence. Except one.

This second year calf was nose to nose with the fence and didn't have the courage to jump. Back and forth it paced, fifteen or twenty times, searching madly for a way around the intrusive green webbing. For a moment, the rest of the herd waited and watched. Soon, the others moved on. Except one.

One elk stood at the crest of the hill, watching and waiting for the other elk to jump. Was it offering words of encouragement, I wondered? Was it impelling, with its power, majesty and regal stature, to the other elk to find the courage to conquer this overwhelming uncertainty?

After more pacing, more fear, more agitated hesitation, the elk cautiously nosed up to the fence one more time. Then, elegantly, gracefully and with the mystery of great magic, found the courage, and smoothly vaulted the fence. At the top of the hill, before setting off in search of the rest of the herd, it stopped and turned, as if to say "I'm doing fine - I'll just keep pedaling".

We all need courage every day. The word courage, which comes from the Latin word "cor", means "heart". To have courage, we must lighten our hearts. By its very nature, encouragement from others can help lighten our hearts and assist us in finding the courage that already exists within us.

Through the support, urgings and reassurances of others, we may find the strength, audacity and nerve to draw on our courage within.

Within us is the motivation to forgive, laugh and hope; the bravado to challenge our pain, shame and guilt; the motivation to face life, to try something new, to be someone better with a healthy outlook and a fresh new approach. Inside us is the courage and patience to look at our beliefs, our attitudes, our patterns, and ourselves.

With courage, we may find the spirit to choose, to pray, to cry and to love; the fortitude to recognize, the prowess to heal and the valiance to follow, all that is in our hearts.

And our hearts know the real truth about where we're pedaling.

Food for thought:
"Why not go out on a limb? Isn't that where the fruit is?"
Frank Scully

Encourage!

Pavlova
Cookies & Considerations
on following page.

Pavlova

3 egg whites
3 Tbsp. cold water
1 cup berry sugar
1/4 tsp. salt
1 tsp. vinegar
1 tsp. vanilla
1 Tbsp. cornstarch

Beat egg whites till stiff. Add cold water, one tablespoon at a time and mix well. With mixer running, gradually add sugar. Fold in salt, vinegar, vanilla and cornstarch. Spread in circles on parchment paper (makes about 10 hockey puck size meringues, or 1 large cake size one).

Bake at 325 for 15 - 45 minutes (depending on size) or until lightly browned. Turn oven off. Leave cookies in oven to cool for 1 hour, or overnight.

Serve with whipped cream and fresh fruit.

Cookies & Considerations:

I encourage you to go out on a limb and make some Pavlova. This light as air, soft meringue is a traditional New Zealand cookie. It is also encouraged that you serve it in the traditional way, by topping and garnishing it, just before eating, with some fresh fruit and whipping cream. The cookies can be made individually or as one big cake-sized cookie - whichever you have the courage for.

Chocolate Walnut Rum Balls

2 & 1/2 cups vanilla wafer crumbs
1 cup finely chopped walnuts
1 cup (6 oz.) semisweet chocolate
1/2 cup sugar
3 Tbsp. corn syrup
1/2 cup amber or dark rum
extra icing sugar, cinnamon sugar, ground nuts or cocoa for rolling

Combine vanilla wafer crumbs and walnuts. Set aside. Melt chocolate. Add sugar, corn syrup and rum. Blend well and add to crumb mixture. Stir well. Roll dough into 1-inch balls and roll in extra cinnamon sugar, icing sugar or cocoa to coat evenly. Cover and refrigerate overnight, or until ready to use. (Will keep 2 - 3 weeks in refrigerator.)

Cookies & Considerations:
The quintessential rum ball is hard to beat and easy to make. These ones are moist and delicious and heavily spiked! Hic!!

"Why Me?"

"Set backs are given to ordinary people to make them extraordinary."

That quote, from an unknown source, may be applicable any number of times - when we don't understand why something has happened, when life knocks us to our knees, and when we struggle through the dark realm of fear, hurt and frustration to find the light.

We generally take our health for granted, so when the unthinkable happens and a matter of health is challenging us in a serious way, we startle to complete awareness and ask, an astonished "Why me?".

The answers, if they come, often surprise us. Some answers we don't like and some, we never find. The realization that we aren't supposed to have all the answers, is one of the hardest things to accept. A serious illness is another.

A lump, a cyst, a wacky blood count, extreme pain - every illness, from a cold, to the flu or chicken pox, from cancer to heart disease, or the tormenting affliction of AIDS, they all have something to teach us, if we are willing to learn.

Most of us have had times in our lives when we feel overwhelmed and helpless, depressed and panicked, stranded in the mire of disbelief, asking "Why me?".

Why not you? It isn't a punishment.

When we encounter our own limitations, we literally slow down and take one step at a time. We mourn the loss and experience the uncertainties of shattered dreams. We can say, "poor me" or we can look for new meaning and commitment, a goal to work towards. Day by day, we grow, move forward and regain the sanity.

Time is a great healer. When the shock wears off, we can discover that the difficulties we encounter, over time, will make us stronger and better.

Life will go on. Some days we won't feel like doing it. It hurts too much. We just don't want to continue. But we do. Somehow, we endure and possibly we recognize that remarkable things can happen if we view our health problems as challenges and opportunities to grow, to change, to repair the connection. We are never really alone.

Irving Berlin says, "Life is 10 percent what you make it and 90 percent how you take it." Find new purpose and meaning. Find a new attitude and face your tomorrow. Be a survivor. Take what you learn and share it. Give others the strength to go through the same thing. Light the darkness for other people.

Hardship tempers the soul. We are here for a limited, finite amount of time. And there's still so much to do.

Food for thought:
"There is no path
so dark,
nor road so steep,
nor hill so slippery
that other people have
not been there
before me
and survived.
May my dark times
teach me to help
the people I love
on similar journeys."
Maggie Bedrosian

Survive!

Granola Bar
Cookies & Considerations
on following page.

Granola Bar Cookies

1 cup whole wheat flour
1/3 cup wheat germ
1/2 cup dry milk powder
1/4 tsp. baking powder
1/4 tsp. baking soda
1/2 tsp. salt
3/4 cup butter or margarine
1/4 cup peanut butter
1 cup brown sugar
1 egg
2 Tbsp. honey
2 Tbsp. water
1 tsp. vanilla
1 cup rolled oats
1/2 cup nuts
1/4 cup sunflower seeds
1/4 cup sesame seeds
1/4 cup flax seeds
1/2 cup raisins
1/2 cup dried apricots, chopped
1/2 cup chocolate chips or chunks

Combine flour, wheat germ, milk powder, baking powder, baking soda, salt. Set aside. Cream butter and peanut butter with brown sugar. Mix till fluffy. Add egg, honey, water and vanilla. Blend well. Add flour mixture. Add oats, nuts, seeds, raisins, apricots and chocolate chips. Drop onto greased cookie sheets.

Bake at 350 for 10 - 12 minutes.

Cookies & Considerations:

We'll need a good portion of these twenty-one ingredients to help get you through: hope, love, courage, love, determination, love, attitude, love, faith, love, support, love, kindness, love, compassion, love, insight, love, humor, love, and love. Measure carefully!

You'll need the next twenty-one ingredients to make these soft, crunchy cookies for those you love. They're high protein and fiber, with lots of nuts, seeds and fruits to help you fight back and become a survivor. Measure carefully!

Zimtstern
(Swiss Cinnamon Cookies)

3 cups walnuts, finely ground
1 Tbsp. cinnamon
2 & 3/4 cups icing sugar, divided
3 egg whites
extra icing sugar for rolling

Combine walnuts, cinnamon and 3/4 cup icing sugar. Set aside. Beat egg whites until foamy. Gradually add 2 cups icing sugar. Beat until mixture holds soft peaks (3 - 4 minutes). Remove 1/2 cup of batter, cover and set aside. Fold in nut mixture. On an icing sugared surface, roll dough out to 1/8 inch thickness. Using a small star cookie cutter, cut dough out and place on parchment lined baking sheets. Ice tops of cookies with reserved egg white batter. Decorate with chopped walnuts, colored sugar, dragees or candied fruit.

Bake at 300 for 12 - 14 minutes or until set and very lightly browned.

Cookies & Considerations:

Zimtstern is a traditional German cookie meaning "cinnamon stars". (Pictured here with no egg white frosting.)

When Life Gives You Lemons . . .

No doubt you've heard the clichés comparing the optimist and the pessimist.

The optimist sees the doughnut, the pessimist sees the hole.

The optimist sees the glass as half full, the pessimist sees it as half empty.

With the summer solstice now upon us, it is with enchantment that the optimist witnesses the revelations of summer, sans the encumbrance of a mighty winter wardrobe. The pessimist, however, may conceivably find fault. Since the longest day of the year is over, it's all downhill from here on in - to the longest night of the year and the beginning of winter solstice.

If there's one thing we Canadians like to talk about, it's the weather - especially winter weather.

For years, we've been apprenticing meteorologists, forecasting the weather with every change in the breeze. Have you ever noticed, though, that when we talk about the atmospheric conditions, we repeatedly give a factual forecast of ourselves?

We can actually tell a lot about people and their willingness to offer their opinion on the weather. On a beautiful, hot summer's day, an optimist might enjoy sipping an exhilarating lemonade, while a pessimist may utter dreary thoughts of parchedness and heatstroke. On a cloudy day, an optimist might smile and say the sun will soon be out, while a pessimist is convinced that the dismal weather will soon have us drowning in the rain pouring down.

Which ever way we look at it, we're right.

Clint Eastwood says, "If you think it's going to rain, it will."

What we think, becomes our world. We each make our own weather. We each determine the color of the sky above us. We see life the way we prepare to see it; we find what we look for. We each decide the emotional climate we reside in, with our thoughts.

Though we can't change the weather, we can alter our thoughts and energy. Our thoughts are stronger than the material world and are shaped by our consciousness. By replacing negative, pessimistic thoughts, with those of enthusiasm and optimism, we can willfully produce a positive energy.

We can consciously reshape our thoughts by what we feel and think, how we behave, what we find meaningful and how we live our lives. When we reinstate thoughts of anger with those of compassion, when we denounce feelings of impatience by consciously choosing to understand, when we begin to appreciate the requirements of others, we use a positive forecast to completely change how we perceive a climactic situation.

Depending on how we perceive an approaching weather front, each dilemma we encounter - be it emotional, spiritual, physical, or psychological - has the energy to bring us closer to Heaven, or closer to Earth.

Food for thought:
"Sunshine is delicious, rain is refreshing, wind braces us up, snow is exhilarating; there is really no such thing as bad weather, only different kinds of good weather."
John Ruskin

Cheer!

Lemon Cream Sandwich
Cookies & Considerations
on following page.

Lemon Cream Sandwich Cookies

2 cups flour
1 cup butter
1/3 cup light cream
2 tsp. lemon zest
extra sugar for sprinkling

Lemon Butter Filling:
1/2 cup butter
1 & 1/4 cups icing sugar
2 Tbsp. lemon juice

Measure flour into a large bowl. Cut in butter until mixture forms coarse crumbs. Blend in lemon zest and cream. Roll dough out on lightly floured surface, to 1/8" thickness. Cut with 1 & 1/2" cookie cutter. Place on ungreased cookie sheet. Sprinkle with sugar.* Prick several times with a fork.

Bake at 350 for 8 - 10 minutes, or till light brown on bottom. Cool completely.

Lemon Butter Filling:
Beat butter until fluffy. Gradually add 1 & 1/4 cups icing sugar. Beat well. Add lemon juice.

To assemble, spread the filling (a generous teaspoonful) over the bottom of half the cooled cookies. Top with remaining cookies, sugared side up, and press gently together.

*If desired, match the color of the extra sugar for sprinkling, to the color of the filling.

Cookies & Considerations:

When life gives optimists lemons, they make lemonade. Now you have another option, or the perfect accompaniment to a tall, frosty glass of lemonade.

These cookies are a fun and tasty, lemon-flavored, summer-time sandwich that puffs and shrinks, like puff pastry, when baked.

Cut the cookies with a round or a heart cookie cutter. Either way, they're sure to perk up even the biggest sourpuss, or the most discouraged and disheartened pessimist. They'll help send an enthusiastic boost of optimism and a message of love to someone who needs cheering up.

Jam Thumbprints

1 & 1/2 cups flour
1/2 tsp. salt
2/3 cup butter
1/3 cup sugar
2 whole eggs, separated
1 tsp. vanilla
3/4 cup ground walnuts
1/3 cup strawberry jam

Combine flour and salt. Set aside. Cream butter with sugar till fluffy. Add egg yolks and vanilla. Beat well. Gradually add flour mixture. Mix well. Shape dough into balls. Dip in slightly beaten egg whites, then roll in nuts. Place on greased cookie sheet. Press down centers with thumb.

Bake at 350 for 15 - 17 minutes. Fill centers with jam.

Cookies & Considerations:

These cookies always bring back many comfortable memories. I don't make them often, but they're special, just the same.

"'Come to the edge,' He said.
They said, 'We are afraid.'
'Come to the edge,' He said.
They came.
He pushed them . . . and they flew."
Source Unknown

What the World Needs Now:
Not Just For One (Day), But for Every One

"What the world needs now, is love, sweet love."

Isn't that how the song goes? And isn't it true - now, more than ever?

Every day, people cry out for love. Singers sing about it. Books write about it. Radios and televisions broadcast it. Children act up to get it. Artists illustrate it. People talk about it

Some people die wanting it. Others live dying to get it. Some take their own lives over it. Others ask for it, beg for it, plead for it and pray for it.

The whole world needs it. We all need love.

St. Valentine's Day is a holiday for romantic declarations of love. Traditionally, most of us speak the language of love, on this special day, with cards and gifts of flowers, jewelry, lingerie, chocolates in red, heart-shaped boxes, a romantic movie, a dinner by candle light.

It's a special day and it's meant to celebrate our love for one another, particularly in our relationships, but also with family members and friends.

We tend to flaunt our holidays. As if we need to justify celebrating love, we create a single day in which to do so. Do we so easily, then, disregard the fact that the rest of our days, we also need love? Should the ordinary days be lived with any less passion?

Is one day a year enough to express our gratitude and appreciation to those we love most? Does that award us the freedom to take them for granted all of the other days? Of course not, but still, we sometimes have a tendency to postpone things we need to say or do, and put off showing appreciation until the next holiday says it's time.

We resist urgings that tell us, on an ordinary day, to make a special effort, to let someone know we care. In reality, when we think of a parent we need to phone, a friend we'd like to thank, a child who needs to hear, "you're perfect, just the way you are", we should act on our thoughts.

It's easy to scoff and delay. We fear the terrifying risk of rejection. We all (and perhaps men in particular) worry that we will give the wrong gift, say the wrong thing or send the wrong message. We become anxious and fret over being too mushy or lovey-dovey.

What we've forgotten is that any gift bestowed at the cost of an open heart has the power to make the recipient feel special and wonderful. When we demonstrate appreciation, we let others know that they are loved. Given with good intentions, the best gifts will be meaningful, poignant, and significant. They will express our love.

We don't need a holiday to tell us when to offer gifts of love because they should be offered every day. A back rub, taking a stroll in the evening, a goodbye kiss, a compliment, sharing a laugh or a smile, bolstering excitement, a heartfelt letter expressing love and gratitude, a "please" or a "thank you" from the heart, a simple, unoriginal, beautiful, always appreciated, "I love you".

Within each of us, there is an unquenchable, insatiable desire to be appreciated, accepted, valued and loved. There is no greater blessing, or gift, than love, and it should be celebrated on Valentine's Day . . . and every other day!

It's what the world needs now.

Food for thought:
"Love doesn't make the world go round. Love is what makes the ride worthwhile."
Franklin P. Jones

Appreciate!

Coconut Shortbread
Cookies & Considerations
on following page.

Coconut Shortbread Heart Cookies

2 & 1/4 cups flour
1/4 cup sugar
1/4 tsp. salt
1 & 1/4 cups butter
1/2 tsp. vanilla
2 cups coconut, toasted
icing sugar

Combine flour, sugar and salt in mixer. Add butter and vanilla and mix until almost combined. Add coconut. Beat until dough is brought together. On a floured surface, roll dough to 1/4" thickness and cut into heart shapes. Place on cookie sheet.

Bake at 350 for 10 - 12 minutes. Cool. Sprinkle with icing sugar to coat lightly.

Cookies & Considerations:

These heart-shaped, crispy, melt-in-your-mouth, shortbread cookies may melt some heart as well. Take some along for the ride. For Valentine's Day and every other day.

"Love is not a feeling - it's a behavior."
Source Unknown

White Chocolate Fruit & Nut Slice

2/3 cup sliced almonds
1 & 1/4 cups coarsely chopped brazil nuts
1 & 1/2 cups coconut
1 cup dried apricots
1 cup dried blueberries
1/2 cup flour
8 oz. melted white chocolate
1/2 cup apricot jam
1/2 cup honey
icing sugar

Line a 9 inch x 5 inch loaf pan with parchment paper. Combine almonds, brazil nuts, coconut, apricots, blueberries and flour, in a large bowl. Set aside. Combine melted white chocolate, jam and honey. Add to fruit and nut mixture and combine thoroughly. Spread into prepared pan.

Bake at 325 for 30 minutes or until golden. Cool completely in pan. Dust lightly with icing sugar before slicing.

Cookies & Considerations:

Not a traditional cookie, but I couldn't resist. And neither will you if you like the taste of white chocolate!

In the End What Really Matters Isn't the Rocks on the Road

In the United States alone, there are 27 million of them - not rocks on the road, but young people, between the ages of 13 and 19 - teens, superposing into adults.

Their clothes and music may be different, but they're still looking for the same thing - their own personalities, acceptance, compassion, respect, admiration and love.

And they still have impossible parents.

As parents, our relationships with our children are always evolving.

As our children change, so must we.

When our children enter their teenage years, they need our understanding more than ever. They need honest, simple, uninhibited caring and communication.

Unfortunately, it's a time when many parents ponder, in astonished bewilderment, what happened to the amicable, devoted, faultless children they once knew.

Our children respond in kind, with amazement and complete surprise. The crabby, absurd, illogical, old fashioned lineage who rule the roost, no longer bear any resemblance to the remarkable, clever, parents they once were.

If our children have raised us properly, though, we can still be helped. With their assistance we can try to understand the changes that are happening in their lives.

We all have some recollection of the difficulties we encountered as a teen. The rocks on the road may be anything from hormonal mood swings, judgment by peers and teachers based on past mistakes, gender stereotyping, emotional struggles, depression, pressure to look or act a certain way, to smoke, do drugs, have sex, drink, commit criminal acts.

Feelings of low self-esteem and poor self-worth, of being completely alone, totally frustrated and utterly misunderstood can be blown all out of proportion, but they are very real and very normal.

Every one encounters rocks on the road. The rocks come in different sizes, and at different times, but they are a part of life. In the end, what really matters isn't the rocks on the road, but how we overcome them and move on.

Dealing with the difficulties of being a teen has never had a simple solution. "Just say no" doesn't seem to work. Ignoring problems doesn't seem to work either. Problems don't get better with age. Like everyone else, teens need to know someone cares.

Start with "I love you". The power of love is it's amazing abilities to nurture and heal. It can move rocks the size of mountains.

Treasure your children. Be their advocates. Show them you love them. When the system fails them, become their system. Fight for them like they're all you've got, because they need to know they're that important.

We sometimes make the mistake of believing that our teenage children don't need us anymore. True, their needs change, but they still require the knowledge that we are there to support and guide them, not only through their teens, but throughout their entire lives.

Keep the lines of communication open by conveying an authentic desire to lend an ear. Open a conversation with "What's on your mind?", "Do you want to talk?", or "What can I do to help?".

As well, both parents and teens can benefit from choosing their battles wisely. Before you get ready to duke it out, ask yourself, "In the end, will this really matter?"

In the end, what really matters is communicating our love to our children and knowing that our children are people we'd be proud of and people we'd like to spend time with - even if we weren't related to them.

Food for thought:
"Turn your stumbling blocks into stepping stones."
Anonymous

Communicate!

Oat Delights
Cookies & Considerations
on following page.

Oat Delights

3 cups rolled oats
3/4 cup coconut
1/4 cup chopped walnuts
1/2 tsp. salt
2 cups sugar
1/2 cup butter
1/2 cup milk
6 Tbsp. cocoa
1/2 tsp. vanilla

In a large bowl, combine rolled oats, coconut, walnuts, and salt. Set aside. In a pan, combine sugar, butter, milk, and cocoa. On medium heat, bring to a boil. Remove from heat and cool slightly. Carefully, add vanilla. Pour over dry ingredients and mix together well. Drop by spoonfuls onto wax or parchment paper. Cool.

Cookies & Considerations:

Today, from my teenagers, I learnt that, what really matters is not the mark one got on a gender stereotyping essay, but how proud I am that gender stereotyping does not appear to exist in him. What really matters is not the mark the other will get on a science test, but how wonderful it is that he has such a joy for learning. What really matters is not that they snicker and smile when their teachers yell at the class, but that they do not judge them for doing so.

In the end what really matters isn't the rocks on the road, but that you get involved and open the lines of communication by sharing your love.

If you are a teen and you feel your parents really are out of touch, and you need to communicate, talk to someone else who cares about you. Talk to your grandparents, school counselors, a friend's parents, or someone you trust.

This simple, no bake cookie is one of the first cookies I remember making as a teen. They've had many names over the years, but in the end, I always call them . . .

Butter Cookies

2 & 3/4 cups flour
1 Tbsp. baking powder
1 cup butter or margarine
1 cup sugar
2 eggs
1 tsp. vanilla

Combine the flour and baking powder. Set aside. Cream butter and sugar. Add eggs and vanilla. Add flour mixture. Roll on lightly floured surface to 1/4" thickness. Cut into shapes using cookie cutters. Place on lightly greased baking sheet.

Bake at 350 for 10 to 12 minutes.

Cookies & Considerations:
A great, simple, cut out-cookie dough.

If you desire to have brown cows or giraffes, substitute 1/4 cup of cocoa, for 1/4 cup flour.

"Age wrinkles your skin, but lack of enthusiasm wrinkles your soul."
Source Unknown

Walking Wounded

Recently, we gathered to remember those who died for our country.

Remembrance Day is a time to honor the war dead. It is a time to remember the hideous battles that define the horrors of war. It is a time to remember the soldiers whose courage, honor and duty meant something - whose dignity and commitment were cherished and respected, especially amongst themselves. Millions died, not only for the freedoms that we enjoy today, but defending the importance of values held dear.

Yet, we are sometimes puzzled. Why do we honor a soldier who died over 80 years ago?

Yes, it is a way to give thanks. It is a way to remember the abomination and vulgarity of war. In doing so, possibly we prevent it from ever happening again. Lest we forget, right?

But how much have we already forgotten of the values of those lost soldiers? Did they really die in vain? Have we actually learnt that lesson yet?

Or is it one that will continue to be repeated?

Why do battles still rage on, in spots, throughout the globe? Though they are not world wars, are the deaths and atrocities any less significant? Is this world peace?

Since the early 1990's, Canadian peacekeeping soldiers have been assigned to duty in former Yugoslavia? Some do not return alive. Is this world peace?

The wholesale destruction of violence ravaged Columbia - is this world peace?

In Nicaragua, El Salvador and Guatemala, a catastrophic disaster leaves the Honduras with thousands dead and tens of thousands missing or injured. A world where many continue to view the suffering of fellow beings without offering to help in whatever way they can - is this world peace?

A world where a few thieve and rob the populace - is this world peace?

A world where food is wasted, while millions starve - is this world peace?

A world where hypocrisy rules - is this world peace?

A world where a child can be abused - is this world peace?

A world where suicide and killing is a simpler, more convenient solution than loving - is this world peace?

I don't think so. Not our world. Maybe in a world with a different value system, but not in a world based on courage, honor, duty, dignity and commitment. Those soldiers sacrificed themselves for a cause they believed in - "never again".

We continue to hope.

All races living in harmony - not yet, but we're working on it.

Aren't we?

*   *   *

We are moving towards a time of greater peace, caring and giving.

If we can learn more about being human - let's do it. If we can help someone when they need us most - let's do it. If we can put hate aside and show love - let's do it. Global problems require global thinking. In order to have world peace, we must want it.

Food for Thought:

"In every community, there is work to be done. In every nation, there are wounds to heal. In every heart, there is the power to do it."
Marianne Williamson

Hope!

Chewy Chocolate Chip Oatmeal
Cookies & Considerations
on following page.

Chewy Chocolate Chip Oatmeal Cookies

4 cups flour
3 cups rolled oats
2 tsp. baking powder
2 tsp. baking soda
1 tsp. salt
1 & 1/3 cup butter, melted
4 cups brown sugar
4 eggs
4 Tbsp. hot water
2 tsp. vanilla
1 - 300 gram package chocolate chips

Combine flour, oats, baking powder, baking soda and salt. Set aside. Combine melted butter with brown sugar. Add eggs, hot water and vanilla. Mix well. Add flour mixture and stir till well blended. Add chocolate chips. Drop onto cookie sheets and
Bake at 350 for 10 - 12 minutes or till golden.

Cookies & Considerations:

The universally popular, Oatmeal Chocolate Chip Cookies - and easy to make, too! No mixer required. Just add love and pass the cookies around. Work towards global peace - starting at home. We have the power to do it.

"The eyes are the landing strip to the heart and for me the heart is where the soul is."
Stan Dale

Triple Chocolate Fudge Fantasies

2 & 1/4 cups flour
1/4 cup cocoa
1 tsp. baking soda
1/4 tsp. salt
1 cup butter
1/2 cup sugar
1 cup brown sugar
2 eggs
1 Tbsp. vanilla
4 oz. melted and cooled, semisweet chocolate
1 cup semisweet chocolate chips
1 cup macadamia nuts or walnuts

Combine flour, cocoa, baking soda and salt. Set aside. Cream butter and sugars until light. Add eggs. Add vanilla to creamed mixture, followed by melted chocolate. Add flour mixture. Stir in chocolate chips and nuts. Drop dough onto parchment or aluminum foil lined baking sheet.

Bake at 350 for 10 - 12 minutes or until puffed and cracked.

Cookies & Considerations:

Don't over bake this cookie. It should appear to be set, but still soft. The centers should remain moist and fudgy.

Drawing Parallels on the Line of the Equator

This year, the 23rd of September marks the official day of autumn's arrival. (Of course our dipping thermometers, frosty windshields, frozen sandaled toes and the falling, golden leaves have been telling us that it's been fall for weeks already.)

As we turn towards the autumn equinox, for many of us, it signals a time of harvest and the month of offerings. The autumn equinox signifies a time to reflect on what we have harvested, but not only from our orchards, fields and gardens, in our own lives as well.

There is a popular quote, from an unknown source. "If you want a rose bush, do not plant a tomato seed. If you want kindness, do not plant indifference. Always know that you will harvest your own crop." Our actions can only be mirrored. We should not expect to reap good, when we know that we have sown harm. We should only expect to harvest what we put into the world.

However, as well as the harvest, there are additional meanings, messages, appreciations and energies, of this very special time of year.

The autumn (as well as the spring) equinoxes also signify balance. They are the only times of year when the length of the night is equal to the length of the day - an equal balance, when the globe is in perfect gravitational symmetry, and the sun is equally divided between the hemispheres, directly over the line of the equator.

This balance is further shown in that, while we, in the Northern Hemisphere, enter our dormant season and our time of gathering the harvest, those in the Southern Hemisphere begin a time of sowing and planting, as they embark upon their growing season.

We can easily turn that into a metaphor for life, since a desire for balance has also been created within our own existence.

There is an ancient tribal adage about the house within us that supports our need for balance. As there are four seasons in nature, it is said that there are four rooms in our house. They are the physical, the intellectual, the emotional and the spiritual. Many times we spend days on end in only one room, ignoring the others. Achieving balance within ourselves means visiting every room, every day, even if it's just to say a quick hello.

We greet another part of the transition into autumn, by feeling the life-force energy drawing us back down to Earth. As we continue to recede from the sun, autumn pursues it's annual shed. Outwardly, the leaves are drawn off the trees and the petals brown on the flowers. Inwardly, we are prompted to turn our energy and focus on the changes within ourselves, reflecting and reviewing our lives.

The autumn equinox is more than a change of seasons. It's a time of sowing and reaping - a balance of night and day - of focus and introspection. As we give thanks for the harvest and the abundance in our lives, we might say a prayer for those who are not so fortunate. As we revel in the bittersweet, final kisses of the late summer sun we might also draw on our love for the rustle of golden colored leaves.

Shall the fall equinox be a metaphor for gratitude, equality, harmony and balance within our own lives?

Maybe we can draw a few parallels. And maybe that's why it's one of our favorite times of year.

Food for thought:
"Fall equinox; my side of the bed colder.
Fall equinox; I mow the lawn one more time.
Fall equinox; the loud caw of a crow
Fall equinox; the first lines of geese going south
Fall equinox; sunrise the color of roses."
Peter Brady

Harvest!

Sugar
Cookies & Considerations
on following page.

Sugar Cookies

4 cups flour
1 Tbsp. baking powder
1 tsp. salt
1 & 1/4 cups butter
1 & 1/2 cups sugar
2 tsp. vanilla
2 eggs
2 Tbsp. cream
2 egg whites for glazing
extra sugar for sprinkling

Combine flour, baking powder and salt. Set aside. Cream butter and sugar. Add vanilla, eggs and cream. Add flour mixture and beat till well mixed. On a lightly flour surface, roll out dough to 1/4" thickness. Cut with leaf, or other shaped cookie cutters and place on baking sheet. Brush with egg white. Sprinkle with sugar.
Bake at 350 for 10 - 12 minutes.

Cookies & Considerations:

It is thought that we should select the best of each vegetable, herb, fruit, nut or other food we have harvested or purchased, and give it back to Mother Earth with prayers of thanksgiving. Pick your best, crispy crunchy sugar cookie and offer it to Mother. She's sure to appreciate the likeness.

Add a bit of vanilla sugar to some regular sugar for sprinkling.
Use parchment paper for easier cleanup.

Tabu

3/4 cup honey
1/3 cup water
1 tsp. lemon juice
1/2 tsp. cinnamon
1 cup walnuts, chopped
1 cup raisins
1 tsp. vanilla
1/4 tsp. almond extract
2 Tbsp. rum
6 oz. (1 cup) chocolate chips
1 pkg. frozen phyllo dough
1/2 cup melted butter
melted chocolate for drizzling
icing sugar for dusting

In a small pan, combine honey, water, lemon juice and cinnamon stick. Simmer 10 minutes. Keep warm. In a medium bow, combine walnuts, raisins, vanilla, almond extract, and 1/2 cup of the honey mixture. Cool slightly and add chocolate chips. Inhale deeply and set aside.

Lay one sheet of phyllo dough on a work surface. (Keep other sheets covered with plastic wrap and a damp towel.) Brush sheet with melted butter and cut dough in thirds, lengthwise. Spoon 1 & 1/2 Tbsp. of filling onto the dough. Fold in sides and roll up the dough to form neat bundles. Place on a parchment lined cookie sheet and brush top of rolls with butter. Repeat until the entire filling is used up.

Bake at 350 for 20 minutes or until golden. Immediately brush rolls with remaining honey glaze. Cool completely and drizzle with melted chocolate. Dust with icing sugar.

Cookies & Considerations:

I named these "Tabu", because that's what they are to the dieter, but you can indulge all your senses with this one. I sometimes prepare the filling days ahead, just so that I can enjoy the aroma a little longer.

I'm On The Last Page, But I'm Still Dancing

When I was in high school, for work experience, we were allowed to choose a field we were interested in and wished to learn more about. I chose social work.

I went into the office in my hometown and asked a seasoned pro if I could learn the ins and outs of social work at his office. I was told to go and get some life experience and then see if I still wanted to be a social worker. Despite being offended initially, he may have been right and I never became a social worker.

Still wondering what I should be when I grow up, I took a career quiz on the Internet. It told me I would make a good surgeon, chef, real estate agent, butcher, rancher, animal trainer, therapist, sportsman, promoter, firefighter, teacher, race car driver (?), or writer.

It is actually through the work I've done as the latter, that I gently realize I have taken on the most "social" of all my work.

Woodrow T. Wilson said, "We are not here to merely make a living. We are here to enrich the world, and we impoverish ourselves if we forget this errand." My "work" writing a weekly column began with the intention of enriching the world by sharing my knowledge of baking. My intention was also to compile a collection of recipes that would result in a book.

Now, as I work on the last column for the book, and as I go over the past 2 years' worth of columns, I realize that, without meaning to, my columns have become a very public avenue for a very individual and personal type of social work. A spiritual journey.

It is said that, to know thyself is the highest learning. In researching material for my columns I have learnt more about myself and my beliefs, my goals, my dreams, my ambitions, my strengths and weaknesses, who I am and who I want to become. My heart has stretched my writing further than I could ever have thought possible. Most surprising to me, though, is that my intentions have stretched into the desire to help facilitate and promote the development of your spiritual journey.

Mine has been a journey that has followed none of my plans and none of my arrangements. It has been a journey I would have vehemently denied 10 years ago. So if you're sitting there wondering, I don't blame you, because sometimes I'm sitting here wondering about something that seems so much bigger than me.

Mine are neophyte views - even to myself. Without a degree in writing or psychology, sociology or even home economics, I have tried to write and perform my "social work" in such a way that maybe - just maybe, if it was written from my heart, you would accept it into yours and listen to your own truth, follow your own path and dance your own dance. And while you may argue my beliefs and my adequacy, you can't refute that what I've written was written of love.

It's true that we each have a job to do. We are each uniquely designed for a specific purpose. Knowing our purpose allows us to learn, from each situation, something that brings us closer to growing and developing into and becoming the person who will fulfill the work that we have been sent here to do.

If I was able to open your heart, to make you feel, to help you demonstrate and promote the power and joy of love and if I was able to strengthen your desire to contemplate a more spiritual journey, then I know that, while I may be working on the last page, I'm still dancing.

As for the writing, I'm not proud of all of it, but some of it's okay.

Food for thought:
"Do everything with so much love in your heart that you would never want to do it any other way."
Yogi Desai

Love!

Spritz
Cookies & Considerations
on following page.

Spritz Cookies

2 cups flour
1/2 tsp. salt
1 cup butter
3 oz. cream cheese
1/2 cup sugar
1/2 tsp. vanilla
1/2 cup toasted, finely ground nuts

Measure flour and salt and set aside. Beat butter and cream cheese. Add sugar and vanilla, beating until combined. Add flour mixture and nuts. Pack dough into cookie press or piping bag, or drop onto baking sheet and press with a fork.

Bake at 350 for 10 - 12 minutes or till firm. Remove from oven and sprinkle with sugar or colored sugar.

Cookies & Considerations:

For those like me, who read the ending first, if this column makes the cut, it will be the last recipe in a book that will be a compilation of some of my columns and all of the recipes over the past two years of writing, including some brand new recipes.

Every cookie book needs a Spritz Cookie recipe. Here's a nutty one for the last page. Refrigerate the dough for half an hour if it helps work with the dough more easily.

"Advice is what we ask for when we already know the answer but wish we didn't."
Erica Jong

About The Author And A Special Request

Cecilia lives in Canmore, Alberta, in the heart of the Rocky Mountains, with her three sons and her husband. She has been catering and baking cookies for the past 15 years as co-owner of a business now called Heavenly Fare Catering. She has a special request.

We never outgrow our love for cookies.
Whether they're buttery and melt in your mouth, spicy and aromatic, or rich and dark with chocolate, eating a cookie created with unconditional love is like taking a little bite of heaven.
Do you believe that cookies can transmit the magical powers of love?
If you do, and you have a special cookie recipe that brings you memories of shared love, and you'd like to share that love with the world, send the recipe, along with a story about what makes it special to you.
It may be included in an upcoming book.
Please enclose your name, address and telephone number.

Send it to:
Cecilia Lortscher
Recipes for Sweeter Living
P. O. Box 8167
Canmore, Alberta, Canada
T1W 2T9

"My kitchen is a mystical place. It is a place where the sounds and scents carry meaning that transfers from the past and bridges into the future."
Pearl Bailey

Index Of Recipes

Bold type indicates a new recipe.

"I may speak in tongues of men or of angels, but if I am without love, I am a sounding gong or a clanging cymbal. I may have the gift of prophecy, and know every hidden truth; I may have faith strong enough to move mountains; but if I have no love, I am nothing.
I may dole out all I possess, or even give my body to be burnt, but if I have no love, I am none the better.
Love is patient; love is kind and envies no one. Love is never boastful, nor conceited, nor rude; never selfish, not quick to take offense. Love keeps no score of wrongs; does not gloat over other sins, but delights in the truth. There is nothing love cannot face; there is no limit to its faith, its hope, and its endurance."
The Bible, 1st Book Of Corinthians

How To Get More Books

Cecilia Lortscher
Recipes for Sweeter Living Publishing
P. O. Box 8167
Canmore, Alberta
T1W 2T9

Did you borrow this book, or receive it as a gift, and would like to get more?
If this books is not available at your local bookstore, ask for it, or use the address above to order.

Please send $19.99 (CDN) per book,
plus $5.00 for postage and handling.
In Canada, add GST for a total of $26.74.

Please be sure to enclose a return address as well as a phone number where you can be reached.

Sorry, no COD's.

Allow 4 - 6 weeks for delivery.
Price and availability subject to change without notice.